Matthew McLachlan lives in Astoria, Queens. He is the resident playwright for Ruddy Productions in New York City.

A Collection of One Acts

AND OTHER THINGS YOU MAY OR MAY NOT ENJOY

• • •

Matthew McLachlan

ISBN: 1535054174
ISBN-13: 9781535054171
Library of Congress Control Number: 2016911067
CreateSpace Independent Publishing Platform
North Charleston, South Carolina

For Dillon Birdsall, who has been my best friend, harshest critic, and biggest supporter (not a fat joke) since I began my writing journey.

And for Erin Dillon, who loves me exactly as I am, empowering me to become the best version of myself, and stopping me from eating my feelings when the writing process gets tough.

Contents

Preface

• • •

Truthfully, I suck at writing about myself. If you ask me to tell you what one of my plays is about, it usually goes like this: "Uh...*yeah*...so, there are *two* people...on stage...and they talk...about this *problem* that one of them has...and...uh..." And that goes on for too long until a friend usually saves me and says, "It's about an ex-convict who fights to win custody of his son from his drug-addicted ex." Then, I point to them and say, "*Yes! That!* What *they* said!"

Maybe it comes from a deeper place than just being unable to articulate my work or getting the occasional brain fart. I guess I always associate talking positively about myself as being self-centered or full of myself. Whatever the origins or deeper psychological meaning, I suck at it. So, I thought that I'd forgo the nonsense of trying to make myself sound good and settle for being honest and open. I can do that, right?

I started out as an actor, and if I am to believe what my parents told me, I was a pretty decent one. I still *love* acting; I enjoy it *very* much and am honored when people hand me a part to read and tell me that they think I would be great for it. But if we're gonna stick with this whole *honesty* business, then I have to tell you…I didn't *need* to act. I think I always knew that, but I never wanted to admit it to myself. Don't get me wrong—I always gave 100 percent and busted my ass doing the work, but I found that I could go long stretches of time without acting and feel perfectly fine. Bad sign. I know actors who almost feel like acting is a burden; they *need* to act, and there's no *way* they're going to go through life without it. Most of those people I know, I am lucky to say, have worked on most of the material in this collection through Ruddy Productions and are credited throughout this collection. On the other hand, I know a lot of actors who *want* to need acting…and I was one of them.

I studied at the Maggie Flanigan Studio in New York City, a two-year conservatory program that specializes in the Meisner technique (and the best goddamned acting program in the city). It's a boot camp for the serious actor, in the best way possible. The beauty of this conservatory is that even if you get through the whole program and *know* that you don't *need* to act, it helps you discover what you *do* need. Like any decent actor who tries to create honest and truthful work, I tore myself apart, searching, exploring, fleshing out what I had hidden underneath, and mining the concealed places of my heart for the purpose of living truthfully and producing good work. What I discovered was a playwright hidden underneath. I took a writing class the studio offered at the time and found myself writing everything and anything into scenes or monologues.

I found a flame that I didn't have to constantly poke and prod to keep alive. It burned and flickered with creativity every second, all on its own.

What you have in your hand is the product of my newly discovered fire, the beginning of me warming my hands and getting comfortable in this creative glow. (I can and *will* drive this analogy into the ground.) These are some of the first pieces I ever wrote or, at least, the first pieces that I am comfortable sharing with the world. All beginning writers get to a point where all of their past material feels like the ascent after lift-off, building up to something better, until they reach a point where they are comfortable unbuckling their seatbelts and sharing their work with others. I will always be thankful for those other pieces because they got me to where I am now. But *these* pieces—these I am proud to show. They have taken me further than I ever thought I could go in this crazy world of theater and playwriting. What you'll find is that my work seems to be split right down the middle. On one hand, I enjoy entertaining people with outlandish scenarios and ridiculous humor, and on the other, I explore the serious human moments that we can all relate to.

I give these pieces to you now in hopes that you will use them. Do *something* with them: read them out loud with your friends, use them in your acting class or for an audition, put them up in festivals, make them into short films, or write scenes based off of these characters. Do what you like! (Just e-mail me when you're done so I can see the awesomeness of what you've created!) If I am able to cash in on any "street cred" that this book might earn me, let me use it to give you some advice: go create. Do not wait for something to happen; *do* it! If you don't know *how* to do it, take classes or contact the people who *do* know how. *Google* it for God's sake! Just go out and create something that you *need* to create—something that may fuel your fire for the rest of your life or just a one-time deal, something about which you can say, "Well, no matter what else I do in life, I did *this*."

I am forever grateful for the twists and turns and for the people in my life who led me to where I am today, who helped me and encouraged me to create. And I am forever grateful that you decided to pick up this book and give it a chance—my little collection that you may or may not enjoy.

One Acts

• • •

Haywire

• • •

Production History

Haywire was first performed at the Manhattan Repertory Theatre in September 2015 for its fall one-act competition festival, placing second in the entire festival. It was directed by Joshua Warr and produced by Ruddy Productions.

ERICA: Francesca Root-Dodson
ALLAN: Steven Meehan

Characters

ERICA: early twenties
ALLAN: mid-twenties

Setting

Set just outside the entrance of a park. Feel free to make it as elaborate as you'd like or keep the stage bare.

ERICA STORMS ON STAGE. ARMS *crossed, heading for the other side. (The first few lines may also be given offstage.) She wears a nice dress and heels, her hair done up.*

ALLAN rushes in after her. He wears glasses, a nice sweater with a collared shirt underneath, and pressed pants.

ALLAN: *Erica!*
ERICA: Nope! *No!*
ALLAN: Please, just…*hold on!*
ERICA: Go away, Allan!
ALLAN: Com…where are you going?
ERICA: *Home.*
ALLAN: You're gonna walk through the whole park home?
ERICA: *Yup!*
ALLAN: Hey…just…wait a second!

ALLAN tries to grab ERICA's hand.

ERICA: Fuck you and your dumb mumbling face!
ALLAN: Come…hey…come on! Don't do *that*, Can we just talk for a second, please?
ERICA: (*Turning on him)* Why…you wanna dig yourself even deeper? You've already proven you're a grade-A asshole.

She turns back around and continues to storm off. He goes after her.

ALLAN: Hey, that's...I can be a lot of things...but...I don't think I'm...an *asshole.* I mean...I just gave the waiter a thirty-seven dollar tip...for two drinks!

She turns back to him.

ERICA: *(Sarcastically)* Aren't you just the sweetest...
ALLAN: Well...to be fair...I only had a fifty-dollar bill...and you stormed out so fast that I couldn't get change—

ERICA groans in frustration and turns to leave.

ALLAN: But I would have left a large tip *anyway. Hey!*
ERICA: You don't know when to shut up, *do* you?
ALLAN: Erica! Just...

He runs in front of her and blocks her way.

ALLAN: Stop for a second. I just...I want to explain myself.
ERICA: Explain? (*Guttural laugh*) How...in *the* fuck...do you plan on explaining that? *Hmm?!*
ALLAN: (*Unsure)* Well...um...(*Beat*) I didn't really think of that part yet. I was more focused on catching you first. (*Impressed*) You're really fast. (*Back to the matter at hand*) But, just let me *think* for a second and—
ERICA: No. *No!* You've had enough time to think. All you *do* is think! So, when it was *my* turn to say what was on *my* mind, all you had to do was say *something...anything* in return...

preferably *not* something completely fucking stupid…but what do you do? You freeze up! You look at me like a dumb fucking cat that just heard the vacuum turn on—

ALLAN: Oh, I didn't look like that…

ERICA: You *did*! It was like…

She imitates his shocked look, as mockingly as possible.

ALLAN: Come on, don't do that.

ERICA: It's true!

ALLAN: Do cats even react like that?

ERICA: (*Eyes wide)* I *have* a fucking cat, Allan! He basically shits himself if I even *look* at the vacuum! And Boots *isn't* a skittish cat.

ALLAN: *(Giving in)* He isn't…you're right.

ERICA: Yeah…I *know* I'm right. (*Beat*) Fuck…what was I saying…

ALLAN: When?

ERICA: Just now!

ALLAN: Oh…

ERICA: Goddamn it. I *hate* when I do that.

ALLAN: I think you, uh…you were talking about…cats and vacuums?

ERICA: *No!* Before that! I said something about…you and… your stupid thinking…and…and then I said something else…

ALLAN: …Me freezing up?

ERICA: *(Relieved*) Yes! You freezing up! Thank you.

ALLAN relaxes, thinking this has defused the situation.

ERICA: *(Exploding)* And *then*, when you *did* speak, you were like…(*Mockingly*) "Oh…uh…uh…I don't know what to say…"

ALLAN: (*Hurt)* Why do you always make me sound like a tired caveman every time you repeat what I say?

ERICA: You *are* a tired caveman! (*Beat*) And *why* am I even talking to you right now!

She goes to walk past him, he steps in front of her.

ALLAN: Wait-wait-wait…can you just…hear me out? Please?

ERICA: Why? Why should I?

ALLAN: Just…let me explain.

ERICA: *Fine.* You wanna explain yourself?

She sees a bench near them. Sits on the end, folds her hands in her lap, and looks up at ALLAN.

ERICA: (*Calmly*) Go ahead…give it a go. *Go* on…

ALLAN looks at her, not sure whether this is a trick. She beckons for him to continue.

ALLAN: (*Uneasy*) Okay…so…um…we're there…in the restaurant…and…we got drinks, ya know? Well…of course you know...you were there. But...*anyway*. We're in the restaurant...and...*yeah*...you...you told me...that...you...ya know...and...I don't know. I, uh...I...I didn't know how to...respond?

He looks at her like a deer in the headlights.

ERICA: ...You're unbelievable, Allan. You and your big dumb brain. Well, I guess it's not *dumb*...you're too fucking *smart* is the problem...

ALLAN: (*Unsure)* Tha...thank you?

ERICA shakes her head slowly, arms crossed.

ERICA: ...I could punch you so hard right now...

ALLAN: Wait...hold on. Are you mad at me because I'm not good at explaining myself or because of what happened back in the restaurant?

ERICA: *Both!* Fucking...*yeah! Both!*

ALLAN: Okay...well...let me...um...let me try again!

ERICA: You want to explain something? Okay. Yes, *please*. Through your *mumbling*...*explain* to me why...after *weeks* of busting my ass to help you get your shit together for your graduation tomorrow, I would be *dumb* enough to gather all the courage I can...and I say to myself, "Well... there won't be a better moment than *this*!"—and I tell you...that I'm *IN LOVE WITH YOU*! And you look at me...with your big googly eyes...and after a solid *minute* of you mumbling like a drunk Muppet...all you could muster was...(*Mockingly*) "thank you."

They stare at each other. ALLAN holds up his pointer finger and opens his mouth.

ALLAN: Ah. Yes. (*Beat*) That's...not so easy to explain.

ERICA: *(Anger still present, but a sadness creeping in)* Goddamn it, Allan. You know all the shit I've been through with guys...

ALLAN: (*Apologetic*) I know. I *know* how hard that's been for you—

ERICA: And *now*? I'm finally comfortable enough to open myself up to a new relationship—

ALLAN: I know. I didn't mean to—

ERICA: And what do I get? I get someone with an *impossible* schedule—

ALLAN: You've been very understanding—

ERICA: Giving up *all* my free time to help you study and finish your degree—

ALLAN: I *really* do appreciate you doing that—

ERICA: *(Almost in tears)* And after *all that*...I somehow... *somehow*...managed to fall in love with you. You and all your intellectual babbling...and you give me a "*thank you?*"

ALLAN: I know...I *know*...and...and I'm sorry. That's not... that's not how I meant for that to come out. I just...I guess

I was a little...(*Searching for the right word*) "Stunned" isn't the right word. "Speechless"?

ERICA: That's just a synonym for "stunned," you *ass*...

ALLAN: *Right*...right. Yes, it is. (*Beat*) I, uh...I don't know... I'm not...(*Getting frustrated*) I'm not as good as you at expressing...ya know...how I feel!

ERICA: No shit.

ALLAN: And...you telling me...what you told me...it's a lot for me...

ERICA reacts to this negatively.

ALLAN: No-no-no! That's not a *bad* thing!

ERICA: *No?*

ALLAN: No! It's a lot because...I have at least *some* common sense to know that...you saying something as big as... (*Whispers*) "I love you"...requires a response...a *good* response. And you know me...words are not my strongest suit.

ERICA:...Are you fucking kidding me, Allan? If I mention *anything* related to engineering, it's like I put a roll of quarters in you. You don't shut up...

ALLAN: Well...yes! That's because it's what I *know*. It's easy for me to talk about it.

ERICA: Well, I know that I love you...so...there's that...

ALLAN stares at her and heaves a heavy sigh. He looks around, trying to find the right words, getting more and more frustrated.

ALLAN: *Crap.* (*Fighting with himself*) It's just…I…I know… (*Beat*) Goddamn it…

ERICA: What…

ALLAN: Okay…I…I don't know…I just…it's like I…I have these…*feelings*…I *do*! They're *there*. But my whole life has been about *thinking*. Neck up, ya know? And you know my family. They don't express their feelings…like…at *all*. And…you and I have talked about this, and I've tried *so* hard. I just…don't know *how* to say what I'm feeling.

ERICA: Well, that's frustrating as shit for me, Allan…

ALLAN: Yeah. I know. But…(*Beat*) I *know* they're there… these feelings? I just can't get them out as easily as you… (*Gets an idea*) Just…gimme a second…okay? Let me figure this out…

He tilts his head down and closes his eyes, deep in concentration.

ERICA: Figure *what* out?

ALLAN throws up his hands while keeping his eyes closed.

ALLAN: *Just…*

He thinks for several moments, pacing slightly. He makes small hand gestures, and his mouth moves. His eyes shoot open.

ALLAN: Okay! So…I suck at telling you how I *feel*, right? So, I'm not gonna do that. I can just…tell you what I *know*.

ERICA: What the hell are you talking about?

ALLAN: Like...okay...(*Beat*) I *know*...that when you help me study...I understand the material better! Even if you're in the same room when I study. That's a *fact*!

ERICA rolls her eyes slightly. She opens her mouth to speak, but he continues.

ALLAN: Now...I *know*...that when we hold hands, my heart...it beats a little faster! It's true, I timed it once. I don't know why.

She squints slightly, unsure.

ALLAN: *And*...I'm normally a restless sleeper. Like, my brain never wants to stop working, even when I go to bed. But...I *know*...that when we sleep together...and you're cuddled up next to me...my mind...it turns off *completely*, and I fall asleep within *minutes*. And I get the best sleep! It's like... my mind can only relax when I'm with you. (*Remembering*) *And! AND!(Beat)* You know how you always look into my eyes, and my pupils are always dilating? You said it's probably from reading too much. Well...I tried looking up why they might be doing that. I don't know, maybe I just needed a new pair of glasses or something. (*Slowly getting worked up*) *Then*...I came across this *fascinating* study...and it talked about newborns and their eyes. These researchers discovered that these babies' pupils were going *haywire* when they looked at their mothers' faces or-or-or…their *fathers'*…but…no one else's!

ERICA: What does this have to do with—

ALLAN: Hold on…almost done…I promise. (*Beat*) Their research showed…that human eyes keep doing this as we get older, and can eventually extend to people we have a strong emotional connection with…and when we're adults…it's not uncommon for your pupils to do that… when you're…(*Finding how to say it*) in *love*…with some-one…(*Beat*) Now…I might not be able to express to you how I *feel*…but I can tell you what I *know*. (*Beat*) My eyes don't do that around anyone else but you. (*Beat*) So, if this study is correct…then…I *feel*…the exact same way as you. (*Beat*) So…yeah. That's what I know.

They stare at each other. ALLAN shifts nervously, unsure of what to do next. ERICA walks over to him, slowly.

ALLAN: (*Leaning back slightly*) Please don't punch me.

ERICA smiles softly and puts her hand on his cheek. Studies his eyes.

ERICA: They really are going haywire.

ALLAN: (*Nods lightly*) Yeah. (*Beat*) Science, huh?

ERICA smiles lightly and nods, still looking into his eyes.

ERICA: I love you too.

They smile.

BLACKOUT.
END OF PLAY.

Men's Monthly

• • •

Production History

Men's Monthly was first performed at The Kraine Theater in June 2015 for Ruddy Productions' New Works Festival.

SPEAKER: Scott Brieden
WOMAN: Andrea Izzy Anthony
MAN #1: Robert Cervini
MAN #2: Steven Meehan
MAN #3: Dylan Grunn
ENSEMBLE MEN: Blake Merriman, Marco Bettencourt Urbina, Pedro Morillo Jr., Sergio Bettencourt Urbina, and Terrence Ruggiero

Characters

Speaker: well put together
Woman: innocent looking
Man #1: construction worker type. A tough guy
Man #2: sensitive, shy, passionate
Man #3: a man's man. A Hugh Hefner type
Ensemble men: any and all types

Setting

A bare room or basement.

Lights up on a half dozen or so men who vary in look and age. They all sit in folding metal chairs that face the stage-left wall, where SPEAKER stands behind a podium, looking down at his notes. They all talk among themselves, though the chairs are all placed in random spots with no semblance of order or rows. They look over their shoulders and turn in their seats to talk. Behind them, on the up-stage wall, hangs a large simply designed banner that reads, "Delegation of United Men." The D, U, *and* M *are underlined. After a few moments of loud chatter, SPEAKER raises his hands to quiet the group.*

SPEAKER:. All right! All right! Settle down! Settle down!

The group stop their discussions and turn in their seats to face SPEAKER.

SPEAKER: Thank you. (*Smiling*) And welcome all, to our monthly gathering for the Delegation of United Men. To you, I say…

His smile disappears, and he gives a quick upward jolt of his head with a deadpan face.

SPEAKER: Sup.

The men repeat the gesture and greeting.

MEN: (*In unison)* Sup.

SPEAKER: (*Smiling again*) We start, per usual, with general news and announcements. First off, a big thank-you to Phil (*Points to one of the men*) for arranging this location for our meeting.

Unenthusiastic applause from the men. One of them men raises a hand halfheartedly and nods.

SPEAKER: Sadly…after last month's debacle at Hooters… well…needless to say, we aren't invited back there for the time being.

The men grumble their sadness and disapproval.

SPEAKER: *However!* I'm being *told*…that there *is* a Wing House being built in close proximity.

The men grumble approvingly.

SPEAKER: So, it seems we will still be getting our monthly helping of breasts…fried *or* grilled, I've been told they have many different options.

The men nod and look at each other, impressed.

SPEAKER: All right. Next on the agenda. (*Looks at notes*) Ah, yes. This coming Saturday marks our first-ever fantasy football kickoff party. As many of you know, everyone here has registered in the league, though most of you have stated that you are unsure as to *how* fantasy football actually works. But I've just gotten confirmation thaaaaat…(*Scans notes*) Yup…absolutely *no one* actually knows how fantasy football works.

The men nod and mumble relief.

SPEAKER: The party will help us learn how to *sound* like we know what we're talking about when interacting with others. (*Lists on fingers*) What key words to say, appropriate player names to throw out, and various phrases and when to use them. It's important that we learn these things and sound like we know what we're talking about, what with the popularity of fantasy football on the rise…not exactly sure *why*, but…such is life. So, bring snacks, a notebook, and an outfit to move around in. All right, moving on! *(Looks back at notes)* Next article of business…(*Beat*) Ah…yes…(*Somewhat troubled*) There have been reports within our community recently…of certain activities that men are partaking in. Things we have already tried to remedy in the past.

He looks at the group like a disappointed father. The men look like guilty children.

SPEAKER: I am talking, of course, about the public transportation *leg spread.*

The group of men look at their feet or around the room, trying to avoid eye contact with SPEAKER.

SPEAKER: Now, I know what you're going to say, and I *agree* with you. But letting the public see leg spreading as a common occurrence only reflects negatively on us.

MAN #1 raises his hand.

SPEAKER: (*Pointing at MAN #1*) Yes.

MAN #1 stands up.

MAN #1: (*Flustered*) Uh, yeah…I just…I don't see why we can't…ya know…tell the world why we do that.

SPEAKER sighs and gives MAN #1 a look. He's heard this argument hundreds of times before.

SPEAKER: *Because*…we men are a humble bunch…and we don't want to look boastful or egotistical.

MAN #1: Right…yeah, totally…it's just…I happen to have… I mean…(*Motions to the rest of the group*) *All* of us have… enormous man bits. And as decent as we all want to be to those around us…closing our legs on the train…it's excruciating!

The men grumble in agreement.

MAN #1: It, uh…it…(*The pitch of his voice gets higher*) It-squishes-my-bits-together, ya know?

The men grumble in uncomfortable agreement.

SPEAKER: I know…I know. And we've tried other methods to appease those around us, especially the lady folk.

MAN #1: I'm just sayin'…and no offense to women…but they've never sat on their own balls before. Or smashed 'em together with their own legs when makin' room for others.

The men agree even louder.

SPEAKER: Listen…I feel your pain. Trust me…

MAN #1: I guess it's the whole thing that bugs me…

SPEAKER: How do you mean?

MAN #1: You know…the history behind it. A group of scientists devised a plan to convince the world that the average penis size is only four inches. That way, when women see us naked, they're always impressed.

The men nod and mumble how that was a great idea.

SPEAKER: You're referring to the Great Cock Conceal of seventy-nine…

MAN #1: Of course. I'm just sayin', it feels like it's backfiring is all. And now…I get dirty looks if my legs are open even a *little* bit.

The men get slightly worked up in agreement.

SPEAKER: (*Raises hands to calm the group*) Yes…yes…you bring up a good point…and we've discussed this before. The only solution I can offer you is, if you're sitting down on public transportation and you're in pain, offer your seat to the closest person. Everyone around you will think you're being courteous, *and* you get some relief to your manhood.

MAN #1 and the rest of the men nod and mutter their begrudging agreement. MAN #1 sits down.

SPEAKER: As painful and uncomfortable as it may be, we must remain steadfast and strong for the rest of our brothers. You all know the motto for a situation like this.

SPEAKER leads the motto with enthusiasm, while the rest of the men are a little disheartened.

ALL: When We Men Are on The Train, Spreading Legs Can Be a Pain.

SPEAKER: (*Smiling*) That's right. Very good. (*Beat*) Okay! Moving on! (*Looking at notes*) Ah…right…(*Somewhat nervous*) This is, uh…*usually* the time when we turn on the projector to look at the shirtless mirror pictures we've all taken throughout the month, to approve them as a group for our various dating sites or social media pages. *But…*

we're gonna do something a little different this month. Tonight...we'll be having a guest speaker.

The men look around, confused.

SPEAKER: Now...with growing concerns about our activities and actions in the community as of late, I thought it might prove more beneficial to have someone who is affected by them address you directly. (*Beat*) So...I have *agreed*...to let a representative for the Coalition of Organized Women speak with us tonight.

The men rumble with various reactions: some shocked, some angry, and others yell because they don't want to be left out. SPEAKER raises his hands to calm them.

SPEAKER: (*Composed*) Calm yourselves! Calm! I know! Yes...

The men quiet down.

SPEAKER: I know you don't like surprises. We all remember what happened when Hooters brought us ranch dressing instead of blue cheese...

The men recall the memory with horror and disdain.

SPEAKER: But I think this will be beneficial for both parties. I promise...nothing bad will happen. (*Beat*) So, let's give her a warm welcome and hear what she has to say. Shall we?

SPEAKER turns and motions for someone behind him offstage to come to the podium. As WOMAN enters, SPEAKER starts to clap, the men follow suit, though a little unsure.

WOMAN carries a small business bag and her own set of notes. As WOMAN makes her way to the podium, the men stop their clapping and look around nervously. SPEAKER takes his notes and moves upstage. WOMAN places her bag by her feet and her notes on top of the podium. She looks over her notes as the men sit there, on edge. She looks up at the group and leans over the podium toward them.

WOMAN: (*Over enunciating*) HELLO…MEN!

The men reel back in fear.

WOMAN: IT IS GOOD…TO BE HERE!

The men cover their faces with their arms, place their hands over their ears, or duck their heads between their legs. SPEAKER walks quickly over to WOMAN.

SPEAKER: Oh! You don't have to yell. Speak normally… they'll understand you just fine.

WOMAN: (*Confused*) Really?

She looks down at her notes, as if there was some sort of mistake.

WOMAN: Hm.

SPEAKER retakes his place upstage. The men slowly lower their limbs and look at

WOMAN. She looks up and smiles professionally.

WOMAN: (*Calmly*) I apologize. Let me start over... (*Enunciating calmly*) Hello...men.

The men all turn their heads slowly in unison and look at SPEAKER, who nods approval.

They all turn their heads slowly back to WOMAN. They all give the upward jolt of their head and speak together.

MEN: Sup.

WOMAN looks perplexed by their kindness and smiles despite herself.

WOMAN: Thank you...(*Clears throat*) It is good to be here. As you may or may not have noticed...I...am a woman...

The men all look at each other. The three men's lines should overlap.

MAN #1: (*Whispering, perplexed*) She's right…she is…
MAN #2: (*Whispering, shocked*) That's a woman up there…
MAN #3: (*Whispering, confused*) We're men, and she's not… that means…she's a woman…
WOMAN: (*Continuing*) I, uh…I want to thank you all on behalf of the Coalition of Organized Women for allowing me to speak with you tonight in place of your regularly scheduled…um…*activity.* (*Beat*) In no way does the coalition mean any disrespect with the concerns that will be brought up tonight. We only wish is to bring them to your attention so that we may eliminate any future hostilities between us.

The men stare at her, not exactly sure what was said. WOMAN moves on, unaware of their confusion.

WOMAN: So…just a few things to go over…

She reaches into her bag, pulls out an incredibly large, tome-like folder, and drops it on the podium with a loud crash. The men sit up quickly, startled. She opens the folder and looks at the first page.

WOMAN: Ah…yes. To start, I would like to address a serious problem that is starting to become a regular occurrence these days—catcalling. Men…this has *got* to stop.

The men look surprised and confused. She starts to go into what sounds like a rehearsed speech.

WOMAN: A woman should be able to walk down the street without feeling degraded or treated like an object…

The men look concerned and shocked at hearing this.

WOMAN: No longer will we walk the streets in fear that we will be harassed by the constant calling out and opinions of—

MAN #2 raises his hand.

WOMAN: (*Surprised*) Oh…yes. You there.

The men look at MAN #2. He stands up.

MAN #2: (*Timidly*) Yes…hello. I'm, uh…sorry to interrupt. I guess I just wanted to say…uh…for all of the men here… that…we never meant to, uh…what was it? "Degrade"? Was that the word?

WOMAN: (*Confidently*) Yes. Degrade. Exactly.

MAN #2: Yeah…I guess…well…that, uh…that's not our intention. To…"degrade."

WOMAN: Well…it certainly seems—

MAN #2: I guess men just…we panic. We see a pretty woman, such as yourself, and we can't help but tell you how radiant you are.

WOMAN: (*Confused*) Radiant?

MAN #2: Yes…exactly! Isn't that…good? Did we do good?

WOMAN: (*Confused*) Good? What do you—

MAN #3 stands up.

MAN #3: (*Confidently*) What he's saying is…we men have learned that women like to be told they are beautiful… yet…when we see someone whose beauty strikes as fiercely as a bolt of lightning from the right hand of Zeus himself…we tense up…and we yell the first thing that comes to mind.

SPEAKER: It's something we've been working on regularly. In fact, we have restraining exercises scheduled tonight after the burping contest. See?

He shows her his notes.

WOMAN: (*Intrigued*) Huh. (*Beat*) Right…well…(*Thinking*) Well…what about when you tell us to smile? *That* isn't the same thing. That only infuriates us.

MAN #2: (*Timidly*) I mean no disrespect…but…(*Smiles widely*) Have you *seen* a woman smile? There's nothing better!

MAN #3: It's as good as unbuttoning your pants at the end of a long day's work.

MAN #1 stands up.

MAN #1: Or finding a trustworthy all-you-can-eat buffet!

MAN #2: We apologize for the trouble we've caused…and we will do our part to make sure it doesn't happen in the future.

He looks around at the other men for approval. They all nod enthusiastically. The three men sit back down in their seats. WOMAN stands there, stunned.

WOMAN: Um…okay…(*Looks down at book*) Well…(*Turns a few pages*) I guess…next on the list then. Ah…of course. Over-sexualization and misrepresentation of women. Men…we live in an era of unrealistic beauty standards for women all over the world. Film, TV, and advertisements are *filled* with images of women that are overly sexualized for the amusement of the male viewer.

The men look confused.

WOMAN: To increase their features, women are *photoshopped* to unrecognizable levels! Everywhere you look, there's some airbrushed this, some retouched that. All of these images…*directed* toward men! Reinforcing your idea of what the actual female body should be like!

The men stare at WOMAN in stunned silence. SPEAKER takes a step toward WOMAN, leaning in.

SPEAKER: Actually…we men don't really pay attention to any of that stuff.

WOMAN: ...What do you mean?

SPEAKER: We're not exactly sure *why* women are being overly sexualized…

The men nod.

WOMAN: (*Confused*) Well…wait…there has to be a *reason* it's happening. (*Pulls out notes*) I have here a very reliable study that shows that viewership of these overly sexualized images, especially in marketing campaigns, are at an all-time high! So…men *must* be viewing them!

SPEAKER: Well…yes…we are…but it's not because of the women. It's probably because we're really interested in what is being marketed.

WOMAN: (*Confused*) Marketed?

SPEAKER: Well…yes. Did you ever consider that maybe we men are actually interested in what's *in* the ads and not how they're packaged?

WOMAN: Soooo…wait. What about all of these advertisements…like…the car ads with the scantily clad women on the hood?

The men moan, blissfully. MAN #1 stands up.

MAN #1: (*In awe*) The vehicles in those ads are truly a work of art. The jealously I feel…(*Motions to the rest of the men*) That we *all* feel…when seeing those lucky women touching those cars…like…with their *hands*? What I wouldn't give… (*In a childlike daze*) So sleek…so *fast*!

MAN #1 sits down. The men mumble their starry-eyed agreement.

WOMAN: Okay…well…what aboooouuuttt…(*Flips a few pages of notes*) Those commercials! With the half-naked women…eating the cheeseburgers!

MAN #3 stands.

MAN #3: Well…as you probably already know…we men have a strict and regimented diet that does not allow for the intake of junk food or anything that isn't beneficial to our health.

The men nod, WOMAN looks confused.

MAN #3: So, when those commercials come on…the longing for those cheeseburgers is…*astronomical.* I mean…the *preposterously* succulent flavor is clearly visible on the faces of those women.

All of the men tilt their heads in dazed craving for the cheeseburgers.

MEN: Mmmmmmmmmm.
MAN #3: (*Happily*) She really looks like she's enjoying that burger…(*Genuinely*) And good for her…I hope she is!

He smiles widely and sits down; the men mumble in agreement.

WOMAN: (*Frustrated*) Okay! Okay! What about...

She flips a few more pages in her notes. She stops.

WOMAN: Ah-ha! Those *magazines*...with the swimsuit editions? Those are selling at a record *high* these days...and there are *no* cars *or* food in them...

The men stare at her. MAN #2 stands up slowly.

MAN #2: (*Poetically*) Those photos...capture some of the most gorgeous beaches that the human eye has ever had the pleasure of gazing upon...

The men nod in heartfelt agreement.

MAN #2: And those *sunsets*! (*Places hand on heart*) *Truly* divine. It's a shame they are always blocked by those lovely young ladies playing in the water.

The men nod at the shame of it. WOMAN stands there, trying to find the right words to say. SPEAKER takes a few steps toward her.

SPEAKER: If I may...who conducted that survey you keep referring to?

WOMAN: (*As if it's a no-brainer*) *Cosmopolitan.*

The men all look at each other for a few moments before bursting into laughter.

SPEAKER covers his mouth with his fist, chuckling.

WOMAN: What? What's funny? (*Looks around, annoyed*) What's wrong with that? I thought men read *Cosmo*!

The men laugh again, a little bit harder.

SPEAKER: (*Trying to control his laughter*) Oh, good heavens, *no.*
WOMAN: (*Confused*) But...there are dozens of columns specifically *for* men in every issue!
MAN #3: Why would we run the risk of reading when we have porn?

The men all nod enthusiastically. She stares at the men, aggravated.

WOMAN: (*Through gritted teeth*) Fine. Moving on then!
She looks back down at the book. She looks back up with a smug look on her face.
WOMAN: Why don't we talk about something a bit more... *direct*...shall we?
Men's...*intelligence.*

MAN #2 raises his hand. She glares at him.

WOMAN: *What!*

MAN #2: (*Nervously*) Oh...uh...yeah...I just...I wanted to, um...before you get into that topic...I guess...I just wanted to, uh...save you some time...

WOMAN: (*Annoyed*) Save me *time*?

MAN #2: Uh...yeah...you know...'cause...we men...we've been meeting for quite a while now. And, uh...one of the main things that we all figured out pretty quickly was... uh...well...we men...we're just not...oh...what's the word? We're not...

WOMAN: (*Sarcastically*) *Smart*?

MAN #2: Yes! Exactly! *Smart!* We're *not* that.

The men bob their heads in agreement.

WOMAN: (*Taken aback*) Wait...*really*?

MAN #2: Oh, most *definitely*.

All the men nod enthusiastically.

WOMAN: (*Surprised*) So...you all...*admit* this...openly...

MAN #2: (*Nodding*) Oh, yes.

WOMAN: Well...this, uh...

She looks in the book and turns a page. She looks for a moment before turning the page to see the next issue.

WOMAN: That seems to answer...*some* of my questions regarding some...*major* issues...

She turns the next page. And the next.

WOMAN: Quite a *few*, actually…

She turns a page, and another, and another, and another. Somewhat surprised, she turns another, and another, and another, and another. She goes back a page and puts her finger on it, searching. Thinking she's found something, she looks up with a large grin on her face and is about to speak, but then, she quickly looks back down at the page.

Annoyed, she turns it, and another, and another, and another. She stops and stands still, staring at the book. She closes the book hard, startling the men. They look around at each other, not knowing what to do next. She breathes a heavy sigh and looks up sheepishly at the men.

WOMAN: (*Defeated*) That's it…I…I don't have anything else to talk about. (*Sadly*) You know…I didn't even give you all a chance to make your own first impression. I automatically assumed that all men are the same based on the actions of others around the world…and that's not right. (*Beat*) I must say…coming here…I didn't expect you all to be so welcoming and understanding of the issues we at the coalition wanted to address. I *honestly* didn't expect many of you to understand full sentences, but…(*Deep breath*) *I…*was *wrong.*

The men gasp in astonishment and look around at each other.

WOMAN: Yes…I know. We women have taken a sacred vow to never truly admit when we are wrong in the presence of men…but you are due what is owed.

The men look around at each other and at SPEAKER, thoroughly impressed.

WOMAN: Now…we women don't usually think highly of men and their intelligence…but that's because we tend to think that you're wrong *all of the time.* But now? (*Smiles*) I see that you're only wrong…*most* of the time.

The men look as though that was the sweetest thing they've ever heard.

MEN: (*Tenderly*) Aaaawwwwwww!

WOMAN: (*Smiles and nods*) We women are a secretive bunch… and, although I'm not supposed to answer any questions… I want to make up for my actions here tonight. So…I am opening the floor up for *one* question…

The men look around at each other in awe. Even SPEAKER unfolds his arms in astonishment.

MAN #3: You mean…you'll tell us…*anything* we want to know?

WOMAN: (*Thinking*) *Yeah…*yeah, why not? Ask away. Whatever you want to know, I'll tell you.

The men's eyes grow wide. They all look at each other. They jump up and gather into a tight huddle. SPEAKER stays upstage. The men mumble amongst themselves, with their arms on each other's shoulders. MAN #3's head pops up to look at WOMAN. He studies her for a moment before ducking back down into the huddle. WOMAN grins, slightly amused. She glances over at SPEAKER.

SPEAKER: This is a big moment for them.

WOMAN nods, with a larger grin. The men disperse from the huddle and go back to their seats, bubbling with anticipation. MAN #1 is clearly the one to do the talking. They all look at him as he gets up the courage to speak. He turns back to the group, who push him back to the front. He gives in.

MAN #1: All right. All right! (*Composes himself*) So…we, uh… we were all wonderin'…

He glances at the others, who all make gestures for him to keep going.

MAN #1: What, uh…what are…women…*thinking*?

All of the men, even SPEAKER, turn and look at WOMAN, anticipating her answer. She looks up at the ceiling, breathing out with the weight of such a heavy question.

WOMAN: Wow…you all really went for it. That's a good one. (*Thinks for a moment. Smiles*) Okay…*yeah*…I'll answer that.

The men all look at each other in amazement.

WOMAN: Well…the answer is simple…

The men all lean toward her in their chairs, literally on the edges of their seats.

WOMAN: We women…are almost *always* thinking about…

WOMAN opens her mouth and takes a deep breath to answer the question. The men, including SPEAKER, are leaning toward her.

BLACKOUT.
END OF PLAY.

The Knowledge of Sin

• • •

Production History

The Knowledge of Sin was first performed at the Manhattan Repertory Theatre in October 2015 for its Short-Play Development Project. It was directed by Joshua Warr and produced by Ruddy Productions.

FRANK FATICO: Evan Hall
CRISPIN ABBOTT: James Padric

The Knowledge of Sin was later performed at the Hudson Theater in January 2016 for the Venus/Adonis Festival. It was directed by Phoebe Padget and produced by Ruddy Productions.

FRANK FATICO: Evan Hall
CRISPIN ABBOTT: James Padric

A special thanks to Joshua Warr for breathing life into this piece as director and for his work as Crispin Abbott in the rehearsal process for the second performance. I hope to one day see him up there in Crispin's shoes. Thanks to James Padric, for giving everything he had in the first run and even more to fill in at the last minute for the second. Thanks to Evan Hall, for shaping Frank into the character you see here and winning the Best Actor Award for the entire Venus/Adonis Festival. And many thanks to Phoebe Padget, who basically attacked me during the writing process, asking to direct this when it was completed. I'm glad she did.

Characters

FRANK FATICO: early thirties
CRISPIN ABBOTT: mid to late thirties

Setting

The office of Crispin Abbot. It could be a large office with chairs, tables, and decorations or a small, cramped, basement office, possibly at a rec center.

LIGHTS UP ON A SMALL *office with a therapeutic atmosphere. A loveseat sits against the stage-right wall. CRISPIN ABBOTT sits hunched over a medium-sized desk that faces the upstage wall. His back to the audience. On the wall are framed quotes and a portrait of Roman philosopher Seneca the Younger. ABBOTT writes in a notebook. He glances at other papers next to him, jotting down more notes. ABBOTT's watch makes a quick double-beep sound. He jots down a last-minute note and puts the papers in a neat stack.*

He opens the side drawer of his desk, pulls out a file, and places it on his desk. There is a heavy knock at the door. ABBOTT opens the folder.

ABBOTT: (*Without looking up*) Come in!

FRANK FATICO enters with a bounce in his step and a smile on his face. ABBOTT glances at FRANK and then back to the folder.

ABBOTT: Afternoon, Frank.
FRANK: (*Cheerfully*) Hey, Abbott! How're you doin'? You good?

FRANK sits in the loveseat.

ABBOTT: Not too bad.
FRANK: (*Nodding*) That's good! Yeah...yeah, that's good.
ABBOTT: (*Glancing at FRANK*) And how are *you*, Frank?
FRANK: Oh, you know...same old, same old...

ABBOTT: Is that right?
FRANK :Yup.

ABBOTT smiles.

FRANK: What?
ABBOTT: Nothin'…I just wouldn't say "same old, same old."
FRANK: No?
ABBOTT: No. I've never seen you this eager to talk.
FRANK: Yeah, well…I'm not much of a talker, I guess.
ABBOTT: Very true. (*Beat*) And I don't think I've ever seen you smile before.
FRANK: (*Smiling*) Well, today's a good day.
ABBOTT: Yeah?
FRANK: Yes, sir! My, uh…my lawyer tells me that I've impressed the judge with my behavior and cooperation… soooo…they're planning on reducing my time on house arrest.
ABBOTT: (*Genuinely*) That's great to hear, Frank. *Really.*
FRANK: (*Smiling*) Yeah! But…that's not even the best part.
ABBOTT: No?
FRANK: Nah. They said that because my ex relapsed again, there's a better chance that I'll be able to have visitation with my son. And, uh…maybe if I keep doin' the way I've been doin'…I could have him on weekends maybe.
ABBOTT: Frank! That's great! Really…that's great news.
FRANK: (*Smiling widely*) Yeah…thanks.

ABBOTT: I'm sure you'll be happy to see Max again.

FRANK: Yeah…yeah, that'll be good. (*Beat*) They'll have to have some guy there with me…supervisin', ya know?

ABBOTT: Sure.

FRANK: But…it'll be good…

FRANK nods slowly, staring off. Silence. He punches his hand into his fist, snapping himself out of his daze.

FRANK: So…yeah…they said, uh…finish up here…with the anger-management counseling. Get that signed off…and then it's the home stretch. (*Smiles*) And, uh…seeing as today is our last session and all…I guess I can't help but, uh… ya know…be *excited* or whatever.

ABBOTT: (*Smiling lightly*) I bet.

Silence. He sits up in his chair, getting ready for the session to begin. He grabs his notebook and puts it in his lap.

ABBOTT: Well, then…we better get started. We've got a lot of ground to cover and not a lot of time.

FRANK: (*A little lost*) What, uh…whaddya mean…"a lot of ground"?

ABBOTT: Well…our sessions haven't really been the most… (*Searches for the right word*) conversational.

FRANK: Yeah? So?

ABBOTT: So, we need to get through a lot, seeing as it's our last session.

FRANK: Wha…whaddya mean? What does that mean? "Get through a lot?"

They stare at each other.

ABBOTT: (*Conversationally*) Frank…what do you think the point *is* for these counseling sessions between us?

FRANK: (*Confused*) The point?

ABBOTT: Yeah. Why do you think you're here?

FRANK: Uh…(*Shrugs*) Show the judge that I can control my shit.

ABBOTT: Okay. Yeah. Anything else?

FRANK: (*Confused*) Anything else? (*Scoffs*) *And* 'cause he fuckin' said so…*that's* why.

ABBOTT: The point of these sessions is for you to talk to me about what it was that made you angry and to understand why you did what you did…to try and eliminate the possibility of it ever happening again.

FRANK: Okay…so?

ABBOTT: *So*…if we haven't talked about it…and we haven't figured out *why* you did what you did…then we haven't gotten any closer to solving the issue. And if we haven't gotten any closer to solving the issue…

ABBOTT opens the folder on his desk and pulls out a green piece of paper.

ABBOTT: Then…I can't sign off on this…

Silence.

FRANK: (*Confused*) So…wait…(*Beat*) What the fuck are you sayin'?

Silence. ABBOTT studies FRANK.

FRANK: So…what…you tellin' me…all of this has been for *nothin'*?
ABBOTT: Well…I hope that's not the case.

FRANK's face turns hard.

FRANK: (*Under his breath*) This is fuckin' bullshit…
ABBOTT: Sorry?
FRANK: I said…this is FUCKIN'…BULLSHIT!
ABBOTT: Well…Frank—

FRANK stands.

FRANK: *No!* I didn't go through all this bullshit to be stopped by some fuck like you! All these fuckin' sessions to have you jerk me around last minute?
ABBOTT: Well, why don't you try talking to—
FRANK: No…no! Fuck this!
ABBOTT: ...Do you think this is helping?

Silence. FRANK paces around the room. He turns to ABBOTT.

FRANK: What do ya want me to do…huh? You want me to *beg*? Get down on my knees and *beg* you? Is that it?

ABBOTT: No…of course not.

FRANK: Then *what*!

FRANK stands up straight and takes a long breath. He composes himself.

FRANK: See? I got my anger issues under control. All right? (*Beat*) What, you don't believe me? I just fuckin' showed you, didn't I? What the fuck else do you want me to do?

ABBOTT: That's not how this works, Frank.

FRANK: Then what the fuck? I've done good, right? I've come every week! I've never been late, and I never said shit that I shouldn't!

ABBOTT: (*Calmly*) That's just it…you've barely said *anything.*

FRANK: So, what?

ABBOTT: That's why you're *here*. To talk.

FRANK:: No-no-no-no-no. They said all I needed to do was come in here, do the fuckin' time, and I'd be good.

ABBOTT: Well, they were wrong.

FRANK: (*Shaking head*) You've gotta be fuckin' kiddin' me.

ABBOTT: Frank…I can't in good conscience inform the court that you've made a significant change here.

FRANK : "Good conscience"? *Fuck* your conscience! Fuck you and your smug fuckin' self.

ABBOTT: That's unnecessary, Frank.

FRANK: Then what the fuck *is* necessary? *Huh?* What do ya need me to say? What do I need to do?

ABBOTT: What I *need* is to be able to tell the court that you're not the same man who did what he did...that you can demonstrate nonviolent behavior.

FRANK: Bullshit. This is fuckin' bullshit.

ABBOTT: So you've said.

Silence.

ABBOTT: I want to help you Frank...and I think that I can.

FRANK: (*Scoffs*) "Help me." You don't know shit *about* me.

ABBOTT: (*Matter-of-factly*) That's my point.

Silence. FRANK turns and looks around the room, his back to ABBOTT. FRANK

laughs lightly to himself. His laughter grows.

FRANK: This is a fuckin' joke. (*Beat*) You're not even a *shrink*...right? (*Turning to ABBOTT*) You don't even have a fuckin' *degree*...(*Mockingly*) "Anger-management counselor." (*Beat*) Couple hundred bucks, a weekend seminar, and *I* could be doing your fuckin' job. It's a joke...this whole thing they got me doin' is a fuckin' *joke.*

ABBOTT: (*Calmly*) Regardless of how you feel about my job *or* your situation...nothing has changed. (*Leaning in*)

Frank…I don't *want* this to have been a waste of our time… and I don't want this to stop you from seeing your son.

FRANK scoffs.

ABBOTT: Listen to me, Frank…I know you don't believe me…but I *want* you to see your kid. I want you to be in his life.

Holds up the bright green folder.

ABBOTT: But I can't sign off on this unless you give me something here. (*Frustrated*). If you *don't*…you won't be able to have him on weekends, and visitation rights will be limited…*if* you're allowed any at all. And seeing as his mother has relapsed, he's probably with a foster family at the moment…am I right?

FRANK is silent.

ABBOTT: If she completes a quick twenty-eight-day program, she'll be able to get him back…and if she falls off the wagon again…he'll be back to the foster families. He could be bounced around the foster system for years—

FRANK: The *fuck* he will!

ABBOTT: *And*…as screwed up as the foster system is in this city, he'll probably be in *worse* homes than if he lived with his mother. He'll be in a group home for most of his childhood and probably be on the street before he's even a teenager.

FRANK: And you're just the fuckin' expert, huh? They teach you that shit at your little seminar? What the fuck do you know about this kinda shit?

ABBOTT: I know plenty.

FRANK: (*Laughing*) Oh, yeah? (*Beat*) Look at ya…with your "quaint" little office here and your fancy framed quotes on the wall. Oh yeah, you just *scream* "expert" on livin' hard. You don't know shit…(*Beat*) Mommy and Daddy probably had you in private school since before you could walk. Stuffed into polo shirts and loafers. So…so *tell* me…(*Beat*) How the *fuck* could you know what it's like out there? How rough shit can be? What *my kid* could go through?

ABBOTT stares hard at FRANK. Silence.

ABBOTT: (*Softly*) You're right, Frank…you're absolutely right. There isn't anything I haven't used in here that I didn't learn in some classroom…(*Beat*) Everything I'm saying to you was taught to me by some other asshole in a blazer. Some dickhead who probably grew up with everything he could ever want…telling us what it's "really like" for people who have nothing. (*Beat*) But there are some things you can't teach. (*Beat*) The foster system, the group homes…living on the streets. There were plenty of chapters in a whole lotta books that we were forced to read for some big test…to make sure that we really knew what it was like out there. But I didn't study those chapters, Frank...I didn't have to. The foster system...the group homes...I was already very familiar with those...(*Beat*) Now...why do you think that is? Hm? (*Beat*) 'Cause there *were* no polo shirts and loafers, Frank...there wasn't even "Mommy and Daddy"...

FRANK studies ABBOTT.

FRANK: Bullshit...

ABBOTT: It's true. (*Beat*) By the time I was twelve, I had been in seven different homes. Some good...most not so good. By thirteen, I was living on the street 'cause I was too afraid to go to the group homes. (*Beat*) I don't bitch and moan about it...and I don't blame anyone. I made do with what I was given. And I don't need to justify myself to anyone...*especially* not you.

ABBOTT takes a long breath.

ABBOTT: What I *do* need...is for you to sit down...and let me do my job.

FRANK crosses his arms. They stare at each other. ABBOTT breaks eye contact and sighs, at a loss. He glances at the portrait on the wall and studies it.

ABBOTT: You, uh...you know who that is?

ABBOTT points to the portrait on his wall. FRANK looks at the portrait and back to

ABBOTT.

ABBOTT: Seneca the Younger. Interesting guy. You probably would've liked him. Smart, funny...big hit with the ladies. He advised some of the most successful emperors in Roman history. (*Beat*) Now...*he* said..."the knowledge of sin...is the beginning of redemption."

FRANK stares at ABBOTT. Silence.

ABBOTT: Understanding what you've done wrong...is the only way you can truly move forward. (*Beat*) That's why you're here...that's the point of all this. Or...at least... it's why I'm the pain in your ass right now. (*Beat*) Now... we don't have a lot of time left...but I think we can still get somewhere. So...why don't you sit down...and let's at least try...

Silence. FRANK doesn't move. ABBOTT studies him.

ABBOTT: (*Annoyed*) I get it, Frank...I do. The people you're affiliated with...they don't talk...that's part of the job. But...you're not gonna get what you want...unless you let me help you. And...truth be told, I don't give a shit *how* we get there. You wanna piss and moan? Fine. Go right ahead. Pace around the room and bitch your heart out. At least we'll get somewhere. But if you're gonna sit in silence and pout? You're only hurting yourself...(*Leans forward in chair*) So...you've got two options here. You can start talking...you can at least *try*. Or...you can stand there...and get nowhere. (*Beat*) What's it gonna be?

Silence. Begrudgingly, FRANK makes his way to his seat and sits down, his arms still crossed.

ABBOTT: Okay then.

ABBOTT sits up and readjusts his notebook in his lap.

FRANK: So...now what?
ABBOTT: Well...why don't we...why don't we start with something simple.
FRANK: Like what?
ABBOTT: (*Thinks*) Tell me about when you found out you were going to be a father.
FRANK: (*Scoffs*) "Simple."
ABBOTT: (*Clarifies*) Easier to talk about.
FRANK: What about it?
ABBOTT: How did you find out?
FRANK: I don't know. She just told me.
ABBOTT: By "she" you mean your ex?
FRANK: Yeah...Kim. She just...told me.
ABBOTT: And how did that make you feel?

FRANK: How the fuck do you *think* I felt?
ABBOTT: (*Genuinely*) I honestly don't know, Frank.

Silence.

FRANK: (*Admitting*) …I was scared shitless.
ABBOTT: (*Surprised*) Really?
FRANK: (*Sternly*) Yeah.
ABBOTT: I just mean…you're a pretty solid guy. I don't imagine you get spooked easily.
FRANK: (*Confidently*) I don't.
ABBOTT: Well, that's interesting, don't you think?
FRANK: What is?
ABBOTT: That you were scared when you found out you were going to be a father.
FRANK: (*Shrugs*) I don't know.
ABBOTT: Well…can you think of another time when you've felt that scared?

FRANK looks around the room.

FRANK: …No.
ABBOTT: Never?
FRANK: No…I've never been that scared.
ABBOTT: That's saying a lot for a man in your line of work, wouldn't you say? (*Beat*) I imagine…you've probably experienced a lot of scary things.
FRANK: Yeah.

ABBOTT: And none of them compared to finding out you were going to be a father…

FRANK: Nope.

ABBOTT: And why do you think that it is?

FRANK: I don't know. (*Thinking*) Maybe…(*Beat*) 'Cause…I didn't wanna fuck 'em up? I didn't have a fuckin' clue how to be a parent.

ABBOTT: Understandable. (*Beat*) What about Kim?

FRANK: What about her?

ABBOTT: You said that she "just told you"…but how did *she* take the news?

FRANK: (*Scoffs*) Shit…she was as calm as a fuckin' Hindu cow.

ABBOTT: Really?

FRANK: Yeah. She seemed to have it all figured out.

Silence. FRANK thinks.

FRANK: Isn't it supposed to be the other way 'round? The chick freaks out, and the guy swoops in? Makes her feel better? (*Shakes head*) Nope…not Kim. She was all breeze. (*Smiles lightly*) I admired her for that shit…bein' all cool like that.

ABBOTT: Was she using at that point?

FRANK's face goes blank. He nods slowly.

FRANK: She started around that time. (*Beat*) Pills. Takin' 'em behind my back…

ABBOTT: (*Gently*) She was using while pregnant with Max?

FRANK: (*Nods slowly, without looking at ABBOTT*) Just the pills. Nothin' serious...that I know of, anyway. (*Beat*) One day, though...I came home, and I saw her in the bathroom, stickin' her fingers down her throat. I was like, "What the fuck are you *doin'*?" And she looked at me all scared and shit. Turns out, she'd mixed too many pills together and was afraid of overdosing.

ABBOTT: And what did you do?

FRANK: (*Annoyed*) What did I...(*Beat*) Nothin'. I *wanted* to hit her. Beat the ever-lovin' *shit* outta her for puttin' our kid in danger like that. Instead...I snatched her up and shoved her ass in rehab.

ABBOTT: And how did she feel about that?

FRANK: *Fuck* how she felt...(*Beat*) She's yellin' and shit... tellin' me all these awful things about how she hates my guts and how she never wanted my kid and blah, blah, blah. The rehab center knows I'm comin', so they wait there with a bunch of, uh...those um...(*Searching for the right word*) those big *nurse* guys; what the fuck do you call 'em?

ABBOTT: Orderlies?

FRANK: *Yeah.* Them. (*Beat*) After *that*...I told myself that it's time to get my shit together. Not for me. Not for Kim... but for my kid. I wanted to do everything I could, ya know? I visited her every day that I could...I tried reading some of them parenting books from the library...(*Shakes head, embarrassed*) I even signed up for one of those parenting classes...ya know? Ya learn how to burp 'em, bathe 'em, feed 'em...(*Uncomfortable*) Even give 'em CPR...'cause...ya never know, right?

ABBOTT: What happened after Kim was out of rehab?

FRANK: She wanted to start over. Start fresh. I was hesitant at first...but I wanted to keep her and Max close, ya know? I mean...she looked like a million bucks. Her face was glowin', and she's smilin' all the time...and happy...she looked really happy.

(*Smiling*) A few months later...Max was born.

ABBOTT: And that made you happy?

FRANK: (*Scoffs*) You kiddin'? Happiest day of my fuckin' life.

ABBOTT: And you weren't scared?

FRANK: (*Considers*) Yeah...yeah, I was still scared. But now I felt prepared...ya know?

Silence. FRANK stares off in his happy daze. ABBOTT watches him.

ABBOTT: Frank...(*Beat*) Do you think you can tell me about that night...on May seventh?

FRANK's face hardens.

FRANK: Isn't all that info in your little folder there?

ABBOTT: It is. But I want to hear what *you* have to say about it.

FRANK:...I don't wanna think about it.

ABBOTT: (*Gently*) I understand that, Frank. I don't want to push you any harder than I have to. But I think this will help you...

FRANK looks at ABBOTT, then back to the ground.

FRANK: Yeah…yeah. I'll, uh…I'll try.
ABBOTT: (*Nodding*) Okay.

Silence.

FRANK: (*Hesitantly*) So…a, uh…a few months after…uh… Max was born…I drive by my place with Tony…my, uh… *associate*. And I say…"Hey, Ton'…let's stop by the house… grab somethin' to eat. See Max for a minute." "Yeah, sure. Why not." So…we pull up, go inside…and, uh…

Silence. FRANK is still.

FRANK: (*Hesitant)* I don't know, Abbott…I don't…
ABBOTT: It's okay, Frank. Just…keep trying.

FRANK stares at the ground.

FRANK: (*Remembering*) The second I open the door…I mean…put my fuckin' hand on the *doorknob*, even…I can feel that somethin' is wrong. I don't know…like…everything seems a little bit off center or somethin'…like the air in the room is tighter somehow…more tense. (*Beat*) I call out, look around…no answer. No one's in the living room, the playroom, *or* Max's room. Tony starts realizin' somethin's up too…

Silence.

FRANK: And that's when I hear the bathtub running. I run through our bedroom and open the door…and, uh…(*Beat*) There's Kim…on the floor by the tub…needle sticking out of her fuckin' arm. (*Beat*) It took me…three or four *full* seconds to think…"Where's Max?" (*Beat*) I told myself I was trying to process it all, ya know? That I was trying to get through the anger…the fear. But it took me *that* long to think about my own kid.

FRANK stares off. He shakes his head. ABBOTT leans forward.

ABBOTT: (*Gently*) It's okay, Frank. You did nothing wrong there. (*Beat*) Walking into something like that…you were processing it all…and that's okay. (*Beat*) You think you can keep going?

FRANK stares at the floor. He nods slowly.

FRANK: So…I'm standin' there…and I, uh…I look around… and I…I realize Max isn't on the changing table…or even on the ground. And my heart tightens. Where the fuck else could he be? Ya know? (*Beat*) And then it clicks… and I, uh…I walk over to the tub…and I look in. I see the water runnin'…some toys bobbin' around…and…and my boy…on his stomach…and he's just floatin' there… absolutely still. (*Beat*) I scoop him up as fast as I can, and, uh…he isn't breathin'. But…I don't panic, ya know? My brain just switches over. I put him down on the changing table…and I, uh…I start doin' those little compressions I learned.

He holds up his pointer and middle finger.

FRANK: Pushin' on his chest with only my two fingers… 'cause he's so frail, ya know? Tryin' to give him air. Tony comes in behind me and sees what's goin' on, and I yell for him to call an ambulance. I'm just…pushin' and pushin' and pushin'…(*Beat*) I see that I'm drippin' water all over him…and I just assume, ya know…that it's water from the tub…and it takes me a few seconds to realize…I'm cryin'… my tears are fallin' all over him. (*Beat*) And after what felt like a fuckin' *lifetime*…(*Smiles*) He starts coughin'. (*Laughs lightly*) He gives these little baby coughs…and then he just…starts *wailin'*. I've never been so happy to hear that little shit yell so loud. He's cryin' and cryin'…and I hold him to my chest. Tony comes in, and I hand him Max so I can check on Kim. Tony takes him into the living room… the kid still wailin'. I bend down to Kim, and I see that she's still breathin'…and I slowly pull the needle out of her arm. She starts to move…and eventually opens her eyes. (*Beat*) For a moment…I'm so happy that she woke up too, ya know? That everyone was okay.

His smile fades. He stares off, face hard.

FRANK: I don't know what came over me. One moment, I'm pushing the hair back behind her ears…and the next…I feel my teeth clench so hard, like they're gonna break…and I notice that my hands are wrapped around her neck. She starts looking at me…scared as all hell. And she's weak… so pathetically fuckin' weak. (*Beat*) I lift her up by her neck and push her up against the wall…my hands gripped as hard as I fuckin' could. Somehow…she falls over or somethin'…sideways into the tub. I keep my grip…and I push her down into the water. I just…hold her under…until she stops movin'. (*Beat*) I don't even remember getting on top of her in the tub. I do remember the paramedics rushing in and dragging me out…handing me off to the police when they got there.

Silence. The memory plays on him.

FRANK: And you know what? (*Nodding*) That would've been right. Me takin' her fuckin' life for what she did.

This piques ABBOTT's interest, though he doesn't dare interrupt FRANK.

FRANK: But…by some divine fuckin' being…(*Scoffs*) She starts coughin'. (*Shakes head*) I sit there in my living room… soaking wet… police surrounding me…and I hear her coughin' up the same bathwater that almost killed my kid. And all I could do was sit there…staring at Max across the room…being held by some police officer…who wouldn't even let me hold him.

Silence.

FRANK: I'm sure I'm supposed to, uh…tell you it was all a big mistake, right? That I wasn't myself. That I would change it if I could.

ABBOTT: (*Genuinely*) You can say whatever you'd like, Frank.

Silence. FRANK opens his mouth to speak as the alarm on ABBOTT's watch beeps twice, indicating that the session is over. Silence.

ABBOTT: (*Softly*) That's our time, Frank.

FRANK looks at ABBOTT.

FRANK: What, uh…what does that mean? For me…ya know? (*Beat*) I thought I did good, right?

ABBOTT: (*Softly*) Yeah, Frank. You did really well.

FRANK: So, uh…what…(*Beat*) Are you gonna sign that?

FRANK points to the green slip of paper on ABBOTT's desk.

ABBOTT: I have to look at my notes and go over some things…then I'll make my decision.

FRANK: Make your…are you fuckin' *kiddin'* me? (*Beat*) I did what you needed, right? I said all the shit you needed to hear…right? I mean…what the fuck else do you want me to say?

ABBOTT: Frank—

FRANK: No! I didn't sit in this chair, listen to your bullshit, have you put me through the ringer like this just to have you turn around and—

ABBOTT: *Frank.* (*Beat*) You did well. Okay? Now…*legally*, I can't tell you my decision *anyway*. I'll inform the court this afternoon. You should hear from your lawyer by the end of the day.

They stare at each other.

ABBOTT: (*Genuinely*) You did well, Frank.

Silence.

FRANK: (*Quietly*) So…that's it, huh?

ABBOTT: Yeah.

FRANK: Ain't nothin' I can do or say…

ABBOTT: That's it.

FRANK nods slowly. Silence. FRANK stands up and walks toward the door. He stops in his tracks and turns back to ABBOTT.

FRANK: (*Tearfully*) This, uh…this ain't about me, Abbott… ya know? This whole thing? It's about my kid. (*Beat*) 'Cause me—I'm an asshole. I don't deserve something as good as him after the shit I've done. I fucked up...I know that... but...(*Beat*) I did it 'cause I love him...ya know?

Silence. FRANK wipes his face and stands up straight.

FRANK: You just, uh...you do right by him. All right?

Silence.

ABBOTT: (*Genuinely*) You take care of yourself, Frank.

FRANK nods. He turns and walks out the door. ABBOTT stares at the door. He picks up the file and puts the green slip of paper on top, staring at it. He looks around the room. He turns and looks at the portrait of Seneca on the wall. He turns his gaze away slightly, thinking.

BLACKOUT.
END OF PLAY.

Online Dates Are Hard to Handle

• • •

Characters

MARK: late twenties
CRAIG: late twenties

Setting

The sitting area of a bar.

Notes

A "/" indicates when the next character begins their line.

The sitting area of a bar. A table and two chairs. CRAIG and MARK enter, beers in hand. MARK in business attire, minus the suit jacket. CRAIG in casual clothes. They are deep in conversation.

MARK: So, then it hits me. This is my *shot*! I mean…I've been wanting to propose a deal since I *started* there!

CRAIG: *Yeah*, man. That's been like…your *goal.*

MARK: Exactly! So…I gather myself up a bit…and I pull my boss aside, and he's all like, (*Grumpy voice*) "Now's not the time, Mark." And I don't know what to do…so, I just *hand* him my proposal.

CRAIG: (*Cringes slightly*) And, uh…what'd he do?

MARK: He just stared at it, ya know? He doesn't even know what to say! (*Smiles*) And *then*…he looks it over! Right then and there! And after a minute or two…he looks up at me and says, "This is good work, Mark."

CRAIG: Holy/crap!

MARK: *I know!*

CRAIG: That's just…*wow*/man!

MARK: Yeah! And that's not even the best part! He gave it to the client…and *they* loved it! They're going with it!

CRAIG: Wow…you beautiful overachiever.

MARK laughs.

CRAIG: God…look at you. Kicking ass and moving up the corporate ladder like that! That's awesome!

MARK: (*Smiles*) Thanks, man. (*Beat*) And I gotta be honest… just *handing* my boss a proposal like that? Just like *boom*! Right in his *hands*! That felt great!

CRAIG: (*Nods slowly, forcing a smile*) Yeah, man. That's… yeah…that's awesome…

CRAIG takes a sip of beer. MARK notices CRAIG's shift but decides not to say anything.

Silence. MARK remembers something mid-sip.

MARK: *(Drinking beer*) Mmm! (*Puts beer down*) How did last night go?

CRAIG: What, uh…whaddya mean?

MARK: (*Rolls eyes*) Oh, *come on.*

CRAIG: Oh…yeah…

MARK: Jesus. Was it that bad?

CRAIG: What? No. No, it was/actually—

MARK: 'Cause you seemed to really like her, from her profile anyway.

CRAIG: Yeah, no, I did…

MARK: "Did"?

CRAIG: No, I just…I don't know. I don't think online dating's for me.

MARK: What makes you say that?

CRAIG: I don't know…I just think that I'd rather meet someone first and *then* get to know them. Like at a *bar* or something.

MARK: ...Why?

CRAIG: 'Cause...'cause with online dating, people can put whatever they want on there or...*not* put whatever they want and be something completely different when you meet up with them!

MARK: Was she a bitch?

CRAIG: *No*, not at/all!

MARK: 'Cause from what you showed me, she had that look like she coulda been one of those *quiet* bitchy types. Like rolling her eyes or mumbling grammar corrections under her breath or something/like that.

CRAIG: *No*, she wasn't a bitch. She was actually *really* nice.

MARK: Oooohhhh...*too* nice...

CRAIG: *No*. Not *too* nice. It was the perfect amount. She had an amazing personality.

MARK: Was sheeeeee *ugly*?

CRAIG: No! She was *gorgeous*! I showed you her profile!

MARK: Well, then, I don't understand the problem here, Craig! You said you didn't think online dating was for *you*, but you seemed to have an incredible time on your *online date*.

CRAIG: (*Searching for the right words*) Yeeeaaahhh, but...

MARK: (*Hands on temples*) Okay, Craig...you're driving me nuts here. If she was *gorgeous* and *great*, then what the hell/ is the—

CRAIG: Okay-okay-okay!

CRAIG takes a breath. He looks around in the air for a moment.

CRAIG: (*Avoiding eye contact*) She…(*Beat*) She didn't…um… (*Beat*) She didn't…have…(*Beat*) a hand…

Silence. CRAIG glances at MARK, who stares at CRAIG. MARK makes no movement.

Zero response from him. CRAIG shifts in his seat.

CRAIG: Uh…a *hand*…(*Beat*) Like…

He goes to lift his arm but stops himself before raising it too high. He looks around, uncomfortable. There is no response from MARK.

CRAIG: Her arm…it kinda just…*ended* in a kind of—oh, *come on*, Mark! I *know* you know what I'm saying!

MARK stares at CRAIG.

MARK: I just…(*Beat*) I have so many different feelings about what you just said—
CRAIG: Come on/man.
MARK: That my *body* has *literally* stopped working properly.
CRAIG: Can you *please* not make jokes right/now?
MARK: I don't want to say my body has been *crippled*; I think that'd/be *wrong* here.
CRAIG: What the *hell*, Mark! That's fucked up!
MARK: I'm sorry! I'm not *trying* to be fucked up! That's just…

MARK stares in shock, with his mouth open as if he's about to speak. He scoffs a few times.

CRAIG: And now you're laughing at me…
MARK: I'm not laughing at you! I'm just *shocked*, is all!
CRAIG: *You're* shocked? (*Scoffs. Shakes head*)
MARK: So…wait. I don't…how did this…(*Beat*) What the fuck? How did…can you just…tell me? Tell me how… just…tell me. Tell me.
CRAIG: *(Takes a breath)* Okay…uh…(*Beat*) So…we meet up outside the restaurant—
MARK: And you didn't *see* that she was missing a—
CRAIG: *No, I didn't see, Mark!* Let me speak!

MARK raises his hands and leans back in the chair.

CRAIG: She's wearing this…really cute pea coat, 'cause it was kinda windy last night…and she's got her arms tucked into her jacket—
MARK: Oh, God—
CRAIG: Will you just! (*Beat*) We go sit down at our table, she takes off her jacket, and we start talking…no big deal. It's actually…it's actually really great! We're laughing and chatting and…it's *great*! Her hands are in her lap, but I don't think anything of it…
MARK: (*Rubbing forehead*) Jesus Christ…
CRAIG: We're having an amazing time. Twenty minutes go by like *nothin'*. After about the *third* time we turn the waiter

away, we decide to choose some appetizers. (*Uncomfortably*) But…the menu's like…that tricky…*thick* foldable kind. And so…I see her trying to keep it open with one hand… and I'm kinda giggling 'cause I think it's cute…like…why doesn't she just use her other hand? So I *say*—

MARK: (*Weakly*) Nooo…

CRAIG: Why don't you just use your other hand?

MARK puts his face in his hands.

CRAIG: And she just…*slowly* raises her arm…revealing what was…*goin' on*…and she just starts…kinda…*batting* at the page with her *not* hand.

MARK moans into his hands and puts his head on the table. Silence. MARK keeps his head in his hands and on the table. CRAIG stares straight ahead.

CRAIG: This is fucked up, right? *I'm* fucked up? For this to bother me like it does.

MARK: (*Lifting head*) I mean—

CRAIG: 'Cause she's *great*! *More* than great! She's like…she's *perfect* really. Absolutely *perfect.*

Silence.

MARK: She just doesn't have/a hand.

CRAIG: She doesn't have a hand…

Small silence.

MARK: Can I just…can I ask…(*Beat*) Was it like…an *accident* or…

CRAIG: No…it was like, uh…a birth…*thing*…

MARK: Did you *ask*?

CRAIG: No! *Fuck* no! That'd be…no. You could just *tell*… 'Cause it wasn't just…like…(*Pantomimes a sawing motion over left wrist*) Ya know? Like…it didn't just *end*. There were like…little *nubs* there, where her fingers were kinda—I'm going to hell, man, I can feel/it.

MARK: Nooo—

CRAIG: Like I can *actually* feel my soul being anchored to a place in hell right now.

MARK: Don't say *that*—

CRAIG: I'm a terrible person! I'm a terrible person.

MARK: Wait…wait. Okay…(*Beat*) So…she never *mentioned* this, right? Like…*before* you guys met up?

CRAIG: No! Not once! Not in all of our online messages or text messages!

MARK: And did any of her pictures show that she/didn't—

CRAIG: Not *one*! I went back and looked, and they all have her with her hand *just* out of frame or tucked behind her back or something…

Silence.

MARK: Well, that's kinda fucked up—

CRAIG: (*Leaning in*) *Right!* But what am I supposed to do? Be pissed that she didn't tell me she was missing a *hand*?

MARK: Aren't you?

CRAIG: I mean, *kinda*! That's like, uh…that's like…a *deception* or something. A freakin' *lie*!

MARK: False advertising.

CRAIG False advertising! I mean…what if I showed up to a date and-and-and…I didn't have a *face*…or—

MARK: Well…that's a little different.

CRAIG How is that *different*?

MARK: A *face?* Didn't have a *face*…

CRAIG: Yeah!

MARK: A *hand* you can live without…get a mechanical one or…*claws* or something…but a *face* is a bit—

CRAIG: Okay, okay, fine. *Face* isn't a good example…

Small silence.

MARK: Okay…so…*then* what? She's doing the whole menu thing, and you see that she's…*missing* a piece…

CRAIG: *Duuuuude…*

MARK: Okay, fine! She's missing-a-fucking-*hand*! *There!* (*Beat*) *Then* whaddya do?

CRAIG: What else *could* I do? I try not to stare at the damned thing, and I try to get past it! Not let it bug me, ya know?

MARK: Yeah, sure…

CRAIG: And I just…I tell her to pick out an appetizer for us to split, right? Whatever *she* wants 'cause I can't exactly focus at that moment in time…

MARK: Okay…
CRAIG: So the waiter comes back…and…she…

CRAIG shifts uncomfortably. He looks around. MARK stares, waiting.

CRAIG: She…orders…*(Beat) Chicken fingers…*
MARK: …Now you're fuckin' lying—
CRAIG: I'm not!
MARK: You are making shit up now—
CRAIG: I freakin' *swear*! I was in the middle of eating that bread they give you, and I almost choked on it!
MARK: Either this girl gives literally *zero* fucks, or she's a complete imbecile.
CRAIG: That's the thing! I think she doesn't give a shit!
MARK: Jesus Christ. Okay, so…*then* what? I mean…

MARK shrugs and lifts his hands. He drops them together.

CRAIG: That's the problem. I ended up having a great time!

This catches MARK off guard.

CRAIG: There weren't any awkward silences or weird moments or *anything*. We kept talking and laughing and… having the best time. *(Beat)* It was the best date I've ever been on…

MARK is taken aback. CRAIG notices.

CRAIG: I mean…*sure*…my mind kept drifting back to the issue at ha—fuck.

MARK closes his eyes and motions for CRAIG to keep going.

MARK: Just…

CRAIG: But after a while…I kinda stopped thinking about it. We had dinner and dessert, we talked for almost an *hour* after we finished, and then I walked her to her car.

MARK: Wait…she *drove*?

CRAIG: (*Dismissively*) Yeah, I know. I thought the same thing…(*Beat*) And…I kissed her good night. Like…for a *while.*

Small silence.

MARK: Damn, man.

CRAIG: (*Defeated*) Yeah. I know.

Silence.

MARK: Soooo…(*Beat*) What's the problem?

CRAIG: Have…have you not been listening to this whole fucking—

MARK: Oh, you mean the story where you had an amazing fucking time on your *online date*?

CRAIG gives him a look.

MARK: I mean…okay…she wasn't completely honest with you about…something kinda big. That would've thrown *anybody* a little bit. But so what? You said it yourself: she's gorgeous and great! *And* that it was the best date you've ever had! She sounds like a great catch!

CRAIG: (*Sighs heavily*) Yeah…(*Beat*) I don't know, man. I guess I gotta see if this is something that will always bother me or if it's something I can overlook. And if it *does* bother me…then maybe that's something I need to work on for myself—try to really unearth *why* this is such a problem for me…see if I can overcome the hurdles that may stop me from being with someone who could potentially be a long-lasting relationship…or quite possibly…someone I could spend the rest of my life with…

MARK nods slowly, CRAIG's words impacting him.

MARK: Yeah, man…

They stare off into their own seas of deep thought. Silence.

CRAIG: Congrats on the work thing though—

MARK: Oh, yeah, man, yeah. That's…yeah…thanks…

They go back to their thoughts. They casually drink their beers.

END OF PLAY.

All in One Box

• • •

Characters

SAM: mid-twenties
GWEN: mid-twenties

Setting

Sam's apartment.

Notes

A "/" indicates when the next character begins their line.

All in One Box was one of the first pieces I ever wrote. And because of Ruddy Productions, it was the first piece of mine I ever heard out loud. As a homework assignment from Ruddy, I had to write a monologue of my choosing. As I was brainstorming, Sam's character kept popping into my head as having more to say, which became *Depression vs. a Broken Heart*. I was asked to write another monologue, but this time, it should be a response to my first, which became *Cool Whip*. Soon after, I realized that what I was writing was a full-length play, which I have now started writing.

Though I loved the original version of this one-act play, it was, as I said, the first thing I ever wrote, so it's a bit cringe worthy these days. So, instead of doing rewrites when I already had the full-length version of this scene complete, I Frankensteined a one-act version from the full-length scene, which is what you have here. A few characters and genuine moments had to go, but you'll get to experience the full story in due time.

SAM SITS HUNCHED OVER HIS *kitchen table, with an almost-empty beer bottle sitting in front of him. He stares at the table, deep in thought. In the middle of the table sits a medium sized box. The four lid flaps are tucked downward. Almost mechanically, he grabs the beer and finishes it. A tentative knock is heard from the front door. SAM stares at the door and heaves a heavy sigh. He picks up the bottle and tosses it in the garbage as he walks to the door. He pauses to collect himself. He opens the door to reveal GWEN. They stare at each other. Silence.*

SAM: Hey.
GWEN: …Hey.
SAM: (*Motions for her to enter*) Come on in.

Gwen enters, holding her purse with both hands in front of her. She walks in just far enough for SAM to close the door.

SAM: Can, uh…can I get you anything?
GWEN: No, thanks.
SAM: I think I still have one of your flavored Pellegrino's in the fridge.
GWEN: (*Smiling sadly*) I'm okay.

SAM nods. Silence.

SAM: How's the new job?
GWEN: Good! It's…it's good so far. (*Smiles*) They think I'm an overachiever 'cause I come in early and leave late, but… I've just been trying to keep my mind busy.

SAM nods. Silence.

GWEN: How 'bout you? You working?
SAM: Some.
GWEN: Yeah?
SAM: A few gigs here and there.
GWEN: Good. That's good.
SAM: Yeah. "Trying to keep my mind busy."

GWEN stares at him, unsure if this was a jab. Silence.

GWEN: Sam…I just want to/say—
SAM: Gwen…
GWEN: I know how hard this is right now and—
SAM: *Gwen.* (*Beat*) I really don't wanna get into it…okay? I kinda just…wanna get this over with…

GWEN looks down at her feet and takes a deep breath. She curls her hair behind her ear.

SAM sees this. He's always loved that. He fights back an emotional response. When the coast is clear, he looks at the box on the coffee table.

SAM: So, uh…that's all you there. There was a lot more stuff than I thought…but…it's all there.
GWEN: Okay…great.

They lock eyes, an intense look, one that would normally bring them together physically. They stare at each other. GWEN breaks eye contact first.

GWEN: (*Pointing to the box*) I should just…

GWEN goes around to the other side of the box while adjusting its contents, with her back to SAM. She stops and stares inside. She begins to cry. SAM hears GWEN and shifts uncomfortably. He picks up a box of tissues. Keeping his distance, he hands GWEN the box. She notices him there and tries to compose herself. She takes the tissues.

GWEN: Thanks.

She takes a few tissues and wipes her eyes and nose. She puts the box down and shoves the dirty tissues into her pocket. Silence.

GWEN: I hate this. I hate this so goddamned much. (*Beat*) I shouldn't be crying. I know that's not fair. But I can't help it, ya know? This hurts me too. You're just…you're dumping all of my things, all our *memories*, into a box and just…(*Beat*) I don't know…it feels like I'm being *erased* or something.

SAM: (*Stares in disgusted disbelief*) What do you *expect* me to—

SAM closes his eyes and takes a breath.

GWEN: What? (*Pleading*) *What*?

SAM keeps his eyes closed and shakes his head.

GWEN: I know how hard this is…how much I'm hurting you…but you don't need to cut me out of your life like I didn't happen.

SAM: So…*what*…you want me to just…keep all your things here, keep everything in order for when you deem it *convenient* to pick our relationship back up?

GWEN: *No.*

SAM: No?

GWEN: I just…I need this time right now, Sam. I just gotta… I need to figure things out! For me. I know that doesn't make it right. It probably makes it worse.

SAM scoffs.

GWEN: I just need *time*!

SAM: You keep *saying* that, but I don't know what the fuck that *means*. You need time! *Time* for *what*?

GWEN: Time to…*figure* shit out!

SAM: Figure *what* out? What do you need to figure out?

GWEN: I just need to be alone, Sam!

SAM: But *why*/

GWEN: I don't/know!

SAM: Just tell me *that*, okay? Tell me what you *need*…what you're hoping to *achieve*! Just give me *that*!

Silence.

GWEN: I can't.

Silence. SAM fights back tears.

SAM: Well…that fucking sucks for me…
GWEN: …I know…

SAM begins to cry softly. GWEN takes a step toward him but stops herself.

SAM: This is just…(*Beat*) The worst part…is that…for days… *weeks*…I'll replay this moment in my head. I'll go through every second, every *detail*, and try to find something I could've said…something I could've *done* to make you change your mind. (*Beat*) It'd be a lot easier if you just told me what I can do…
GWEN: I'm sorry, Sam.
SAM:…So, that's it…(*Beat*) I'm…I'm fucking *helpless* here…

GWEN avoids eye contact. Silence.

SAM: Just…if it's over…just say it, okay?
GWEN: I don't *know* if it's over, Sam.
SAM: What does your gut tell you?
GWEN: (*Searching*) I don't know. I want to give you an answer here, but I don't have one.
SAM: *Just*…don't think about it…okay? Just say whether your gut feels like this is over.

GWEN: I don't know! I don't…I don't *think* so! (*Beat*) I don't *want* it to be!

SAM: You think that this might still work out?

GWEN: I can't say if it/will or…

SAM: I don't expect you to know for *certain*; I just want your gut feeling!

They stare at each other, another deep and passionate stare.

GWEN: (*Whispering*) Yes. (*Beat*) I think it will…

SAM: Orion?

GWEN stares at him seriously.

GWEN: I can't say that—

SAM: If it's true, you'll say that. You'll say "*Orion*, I think it will still work out."

GWEN: Don't make me say that—

SAM: If you say *Orion*, I'll know you're telling the truth.

GWEN: I can't say that because I've never broken an *Orion* before, and…and I *don't/know*!

SAM: I *just* want you to—

GWEN: I DON'T KNOW, SAM!

SAM rears back. GWEN starts to cry. SAM turns away from her, composing himself.

GWEN: I should go…

GWEN closes the flaps, picks up the box, and goes to the door. She stops in front of the door, turning to SAM.

GWEN: I know this isn't fair of me to say...I know *everything* I'm doing right now isn't fair...(*Beat*) But I *do* love you, Sam. And that's why this is so hard for me, because...I *know* I need this time right now and...I love you so much... I *really, really* do.

SAM turns. He slowly walks over to GWEN. With every step he takes, GWEN tenses up.

He stops in front of her, the box between them. GWEN looks at him, vulnerable in the close proximity. He slowly leans in, reaches past her, and opens the door.

SAM: Good-bye, Gwen.
GWEN: (*Holding back tears*) ...Good-bye, Sam...

GWEN turns and quickly walks out. SAM stands still, staring at where GWEN was, holding the door wide open with his hand. He shuts it slowly. He leans with both palms against the door and rests his forehead on it. He begins to cry. He hits his head against the door a few times. He keeps his head against the door as the lights fall.

BLACKOUT.
END OF PLAY.

Monologues

• • •

Serious Talk

• • •

Production History

Serious Talk was first performed at Ruddy Readings in April 2015 for Ruddy

Productions. It was directed by Chelsea Long.

PERSON: Scott Brieden

Characters

PERSON: any age. Male or female.

PERSON WALKS IN QUICKLY, QUITE peeved, though maintaining their cool.

PERSON: Dave? We really need to talk. (*Deep breath*) I know you're only trying to be funny...just trying to haves some laughs with the guys in the break room...but when it's at my expense, or anyone *else's* for that matter...it's not funny. With that being *said*, I just wanted straighten this out, okay? Clear the air. (*Points*) I...did *not...fart.* Yeah-yeah-yeah, you were trying to get a laugh. Ha-ha, I get it. But you and I *both* know that it was the chair cushion that squeaked! It's fucking *impossible* to recreate the same fart-sounding squeak when under pressure like that! 'Cause you get nervous or-or-or you apply too much pressure 'cause you're so fucking *anxious* to prove your innocence! And then, you just end up looking like you're making excuses! That's exactly what happened, Dave! And you know it! (*Laughs heavily, clearly faking*) And *trust* me...if I *did* fart...you'd *know.* I've been known to clear subway cars in my day, Dave, so...some petty duck quack of a fart is child's play. *Pathetic* even. And you know *what*! This is not even something to *joke* about! There are some *serious* medical conditions out there that involve involuntary gaseous release. I mean... you don't know what someone is going through, okay? They could be walking through life, accidentally farting with every step, and there *you* are...gettin' your *jollies* on at their expense! And *besides*! Do you know how *unhealthy* it is to hold your farts in? *Hm?* I didn't think so!

Pulls out a folded piece of paper from a pocket. Unfolds it. Holds it in front at arm's length, with a hand on each side.

According to a very credible online medical blog…it states that, "Holding in flatulence may lead to pathological distention of the bowels"…

Looks up as if to say, "Are you hearing this?"

"Symptoms include lower abdominal pain, tearing of the interior colon walls…" (*Raises voice for emphasis*) "and could lead to a process called paradoxical diarrhea."

Puts the paper down and stares at Dave.

I don't know about *you*, Dave…but any medical term that has the word "paradox" in the title does *not* sound appealing…

Folds up paper and smugly puts it away.

So…*Dave*…what do you have to say for yourself? Hm?

Stares at Dave. Looks confused, sniffing the air.

Did…did you just…fart? (*Nods slowly, genuinely*) Good for you, Dave…(*Points at Dave*) And good *for* you…

Brooklyn Boys

• • •

Production History

Brooklyn Boys was first performed at Ruddy Readings in April 2015 for Ruddy

Productions. It was directed by Anna Loyd Bradshaw.

TRISH: Katie Healy

Characters

TRISH: late twenties or early thirties.

TRISH: Hey! You! Yeah...*you*! (*Beat*) Not *you*, ya jackass... turn around! (*Points*)
You! (*Beat*) Do you see me over there? Sittin' by myself at that table? Huh? That's one-uh- them rhetorical questions, ya dick- hole...I *know* you see me over there. Wha's the matter, ya legs broke? Huh? You think I got all dolled up like this to sit by myself? I could be at home right now with my cats, eatin' chocolate and watchin' some bullshit on Bravo. But nooo. Here I am. And ya know what? This is the third bar tonight I've sat at, twiddlin' my fuckin' thumbs, waitin' for one-uh-ya hipster boys to buy me a drink. *Third!* If I stuck to one of my *reguluh* spots, the boys'd be breakin' chairs over each other's fuckin' *heads* over who could buy me the first round! All my friends said, "Trish, you gotta getchya ass down to Williamsburg! All the boys there are hairy and muscular, and they'll write poems aboutchya and shit!" So I thought, "What the hell," right? Why not see what all the fuss is about. Head down here and find me one of the few decent smellin' fellas in this shithole. Turns out, you'd all rather sit at the bar and write in ya little journals like thirteen-year-old girls than buy a pretty lady a *drink*! (*Shakes head, disgusted*) You hipster boys...with ya tight pants and ya junk all in our faces... lookin' like ya tryna' smuggle a cucumber in a Ziploc bag. You know what the *real* problem is?

Looks frustrated and wiggles her butt uncomfortably.

Sonuva...

Pulls on the side of her dress. Moves her butt around in large motions.

This dress is so fuckin' tight…it's like my ass is tryna eat it.

Gives a little butt shake.

You know what the problem is? It's not jus' that Brooklyn's been taken over by you bike ridin', mustache wearin', dumpster divin' *hippies*…it's more that it's changed *so much*. Ya know what Brooklyn *used* to be like? (*Guttural laugh*) It was pure *Mafia* shit, my friend! People shootin' each other on their lunch breaks, knife fights jus' cuz youz were *bored*. Hell, you couldn't walk half a block without trippin' over some body part or some shit. It took a *man* to live in this parta town. But now, all ya need is a fixed-gear bike and some bisexual tendencies. (*Rolls eyes*) Oh, don't try to get all heterosexual on me now, bitch. (*Beat*) And what the fuck are you drinkin'? A PBR? I know you *look* homeless, but for God's sake, man, have some fuckin' *class*!
Lord knows ya spendin' thousands of dollars to live 'round here; at least *drink* like ya live indoors. Throw that shit out, put your diary away, and order somethin' a *man* would drink. (*To bartender*) Hey! Barkeep! This kindly gentleman would like to order a *real* drink. (*Looks back at hipster*) Jack and ginger ale? Eh, okay… step in the right direction, I suppose. (*Beat*) Whoa-whoa…where the fuck is *mine*?

Depression vs. a Broken Heart

• • •

Production History

Depression vs. a Broken Heart was first performed at Ruddy Readings in April 2015 for Ruddy Productions. It was directed by Anna Loyd Bradshaw.

SAM: Eric Kuehnemann

Characters

SAM: mid-twenties

SAM: I'm not depressed! I'm brokenhearted! There's a difference! You can take medicine for depression, fix the imbalance. This isn't that easy, okay? That's why the song's called "How Can You Mend a Broken Heart" and not "How Can You Balance Your Serotonin Levels." Don't you think if I could fix it, I would? I've done *everything*! *Booze, exercise*, writing out how I fuckin' *feel*! But all this just *slingshots* me back to the reality...*that I feel like shit!* (*Sighs*) I just...(*Beat*) There are just so many things that keep reopening the wound for me...little jabs that I don't even expect, ya know? Out of the blue. And it happens *every day*... every *minute* really. Like...(*Scoffs*) Okay...this will sound really stupid...*and* make me look weirder than I already do, but...(*Beat*) When we were together, we'd always camp out in my bed...for *hours*. Just *talking* and *laughing*. And out of the blue...we'd give each other this...*look*. We could be in the middle of a conversation, and all of a sudden, we'd just *collide*, like two magnets, ya know? Unable to keep our hands off each other. I mean, clothes everywhere, blankets all tangled, us rolling around...it was...it was fuckin' *great*. (*Beat*) So...uh...after we were finished...I'd put on some shorts or whatever...go to the bathroom...and, uh... (*Smiles lightly*) Nine times outta ten...I'd find one of her hairs...in my butt crack. No, seriously! I would feel it there when I walked! Then, when I got to the bathroom, I'd have to pull it out! And *goddamn* did it tickle! She had the longest hair of anyone I've ever been with...so it felt like an *eternity* when I'd pull it out. And her hair shed everywhere, so it could have been *days* after she'd been at my place, and I would *still* pick out hairs.

Stares off with a smile, which fades.

So...we break up...and I, uh...I *do*...whatever I *can* to make myself forget...to feel *better*...'Cause that's what you're supposed to do...whatever you *can*. And...seeing as everything *else* wasn't working...I tried something different...and I slept with someone. (*Beat*) Afterward, I, uh...I go to the bathroom...and...(*Scoffs with a shake of his head*) There it *is*...that familiar sensation! And I *know* that I'm going to have to pull this fucker out of there...(*Beat*) And...I do...and...(*Beat*) It doesn't *tickle*...it doesn't make me *smile*...(*Beat*) It tears my fucking heart to pieces. And I start *crying*...right there, in this stranger's bathroom!

Silence. Shakes head.

Now...if there's *medicine* I can take to stop stupid shit like *that* from happening...to make me not feel this way, sign me up, man. 'Cause I'm fuckin' over it.

Cool Whip

• • •

Characters

SCOTT: mid-twenties

SCOTT: Listen…I get where you're coming from…*really*, I do. But…aren't you *tired* of feeling like shit all the time? I mean…the longer you go *on* and *on* about it, the more it'll stir up the bullshit and make you feel worse! You gotta give yourself permission to just be happy with yourself, ya know? Be in the moment! That doesn't mean the feelings are gonna go away overnight. Hell, you'll probably be in a dark place for a *long* time. I'm talkin' like…*awful*, *soul-crushing*, Lars Von *Trier* kinda dark. But…I don't know…*Get out there*…ya know? (*Rolling eyes.*) Yeah, okay, that sounds stupid. But…like…(*Thinks*) Okay…I had my heart broken, right? Who hasn't? But this one was *bad.* I barely left my apartment for, like, a *week* straight. I just moped around, all grumpy and sad…sulked on the couch and ate tubs of Cool Whip with a spoon. (*Nods with eyes closed*) Yeah, I know. But…one night after work, I was on the train going home, maybe eight stops from my place… and…I don't know what it was. I just…*stood* up…and got off the train. I'd never been in that area before in my *life.* I walked and walked…probably for a good half mile, not knowing *where* the hell I was going. Then I found a bar that just…*seemed* right, ya know? Like…I was *supposed* to go in. I sat down, ordered a drink, and watched some bullshit on TV. I sat there…and allowed myself to be in the moment, ya know? (*Leans in*) And you know what happened next? (*Beat*) Nothing. *Nothing* happened. I didn't pick someone up, I didn't meet new people, and I didn't have some *crazy* life-changing moment of solitude. I just…*allowed* myself to get away from my sadness and to be *okay*. Even for a moment. (*Beat*) My *point*…is that you have to give yourself *permission*. You have to allow yourself to be okay, ya know? Yeah, sure, time will help…but it can only do so much! You have to just…let go…even for a moment…and try to be happy with *you* and enjoy *you*. (*Beat*) And if that doesn't work, you can always try Cool Whip.

Women

• • •

Production History

Women was first performed at Ruddy Readings in April 2015 for Ruddy Productions. It was directed by Hillel Meltzer.

GUY: Robert Cervini

Characters

GUY: thirties

GUY If I've told ya once, I've told ya a thousand times. *Stay... away...*from *women.* Sure...sometimes ya need to get your rocks off, and that's fine! Tear it up, champ! But once you're done...*get-the-fuck-outta-there!* 'Cause I'll tell ya what...women? They're sharks, my friend. *Especially* with guys like you. They can smell your sensitive little heart bleedin' in the water from a mile away. They'll circle ya for a little bit, wear ya down, and then...*they chomp down on that shit!* (*Makes quick biting noises while turning his head from side to side.*)

Ahn-ahn-ahn-ahn-ahn-ahn-ahn. And before you know it, you're torn to smithereens...all pouty and shit, like, "Oooohhhh, I'm so sad and hurt! Why can't these she-sharks see I'm one of the nice guys?" Well, let me tell ya somethin'...that's how it works: evil women turn nice guys into assholes, who, in turn, break vulnerable girls' hearts, turning *them* into evil women! Circle of life kinda shit! And don't even *try* to figure women out. They're the most complex species on the planet! One minute, they're happy; the next, they're cryin'; another minute, they're throwin' your favorite sports jerseys in the fireplace because they *think*, in a *dream*, you cheated on them with their sister. And don't even get me *started* on vaginas, my friend. They make no fuckin' sense! I read an article about these fuckers, and I'll tell ya, I ended up bein' *more* confused than when I started. I mean...a *dick* is the easiest thing in the world. You touch it, it grows; you touch it again, *waterworks*! *Wham-bam-done!* A *vagina*? That shit is a riddle wrapped in an enigma! You have to be a member of Daft Punk to get that shit to work properly.

Pantomimes working a DJ table.

Touch this, rub that, twist those. And good *luck* trying to find the G-spot. Tryin' to find *that* shit makes me feel like Jack Nicholson at the end of *The Shining*... running around a maze in a panic. (*Thinks*) Minus the murderous rage...*and* the ax...*and* freezing to death—okay, maybe that's not the best example, but you get what I'm sayin', right? The article *did* have one thing in there that piqued my interest. Excuse me while I get all scientific on ya. Ya know how vaginas get all wet and shit...ya know...when they're hot and bothered? Well, that wetness is called squalene...(*Nods*) Yeah...I bet you didn't even know that was a word. According to this article, *squalene* is an organic compound found mostly in plants, though found in the organs of certain small animals. Not many larger species create this stuff...(*Beat*) Wanna take a *wild* guess at what larger species *does* produce squalene? (*Hits back of hand in open palm with each syllable*) Fuck-ing-*sharks!*

Throws arms up.

Sharks! I can't make this shit up, man!

Takes a deep breath and composes himself.

Will ya just...will ya listen to me...for once? This is good advice I'm givin' ya here. 'Cause I hate seein' ya hurt. Take a little time to compose yourself, toughen up that squishy little heart of yours, and *then* jump back in the water. (*Thinks*) Or…you can always go gay. (*Shrugs*) Your choice.

Ghosting

• • •

Characters

WOMAN: twenties/thirties

WOMAN: He's not gonna call back, Mother! That's what people do now…they just *drop* you whenever they're done with you. It's called ghosting. Yeah, *ghosting*. Like Casper. It's when someone *appears* to be a decent person, but is, in fact, a complete and utter waste of human existence. They take you out for dinner once or twice, show you a good time…(*Under breath*) Maybe gets you to go to bases you wouldn't normally *get* to on a second date…and then *bam*! They're *gone*! They're like, uh…um…oh man, I can't really think of a good analogy here…they're like, uh…
(*Thinks*) Oh! You know the leprechaun money in *Harry Potter*? How it disappears after a few—never mind; you don't know what I'm talking about. They *vanish* is what I'm saying. Blame it on the technological age; I don't know! Didn't people do that kinda stuff back in your day after you'd gone out for…*tea* or whatever? *I* don't know. I thought you got tea! *Okay! Sorry! No tea! Aaaannnyway!* You go out with someone a few times, you seem to be having fun, and then they stop talking to you. *Yeah*. No confrontation, no breaking it off…just…*poof*! *Gone*…like, uh…uh…(*Thinking*) Jesus *Christ*, I *cannot* think of *anything* to compare this to…
(*Beat*) *Yes*, Mother, it *is* important! This kinda stuff is my *thing*! Okay-okay. Forget the analogies! You wanna know the *worst* part about ghosting? (*Bitter, guttural laugh*) The *worst* part…is if you ever confront the person about it, they'll always spout something like…(*All in one breath*) "Oh, *heeeey*! Sorry about not getting back to you! I've just

been really busy! I mean…I know that texting takes *literally* seconds to do…but I seemed to have forgotten that you're a person with *feelings* 'cause I'm a soulless cretin who never felt the loving embrace of their parents. *Otherwise,* they would have taught me how to be a decent human being and not act like a complete and utter *shit* bag!"

Gasps for breath. Breathes heavily. Looks around angrily. Her attention turns to something her mother says.

What? (*Beat*) Have…have *I* ever…(*Laughs guiltily*) I mean…(*Beat*) Not on *purpose.*

Thank You

• • •

Production History

Thank You was first performed at Ruddy Readings in April 2015 for Ruddy Productions.

It was directed by Chelsea Long.

PERSON: Jewells Blackwell

Characters

PERSON: any age. Male or female.

Smiles sadly. Look down at the ground.

PERSON: You know, uh…I've…I've really missed reading your work. It always meant a lot that you'd show me something as soon as you finished it. And *this*…God…I think this is the first piece of yours I've read in…I don't know…two years? It was nice reading your words again.

Holds up an open copy of Vanity Fair.

And holy *shit…Vanity Fair*? You should be proud! Seriously. I know everyone else is…(*Beat*) And this piece…it's, uh…it's good…*really* good…

Silence.

You know…any time you had me read one of your pieces…I always did this thing where…I would read the title, read your name below it, and then take a breath…hoping that what I read next would be this…I don't know…romantic description of how you felt about me…about *us*. I know that's kinda selfish. But…I couldn't help but hope, ya know? Hell, it didn't even have to be that…just something that showed that I was on your mind. (*Beat*) Again and again, I would read something of yours with this hope. Reading into every line…every word…trying to find any hint of me in there…

Silence..

When someone told me that you were published, I thought I'd check it out. I didn't even bother with my old routine. I figured I'd already know the piece… (*Beat*) But I didn't know it. And after a few lines…I started recognizing things. And that's…that's when I realized…(*Nods slowly*) You finally did it.(*Beat*) At first, I couldn't believe it…and, all of a sudden…that old desire started coming back…and I started getting kind of excited, ya know? (*Laughs lightly and shakes head*) But then…I realized *what* it was I was reading. That you still think about me. That you often wonder what I'm doing. How you described our relationship and how you hurt me. I mean…everything about *me* was positive and it sounded *great*, but…(*Beat*) It was bullshit. You were justifying why you were better off. And…the worst part is…you painted yourself as this…*tragic figure* who knows you've done wrong…who hurt this *poor sap* of a person, but…*guess what*? *You're* still the good guy! I mean…who doesn't relate to hurting someone else, right? And if this person doesn't understand and forgive you…especially after you "poured your heart out" like this for everyone to see…then it's their fault…they're wrong for not being the bigger person. (*Scoffs lightly. Laughs.*) But my favorite part…my *favorite* part…(*Reads from the* Vanity Fair.) "And when you lie with your soul mate in the warmth of your bed…

you will think of me…and *thank me*…for all of the pain I have caused you." (*Beat*) I'll thank you…

Silence.

After all that time with you…I wondered what would finally get your attention…(*Beat*) It took you breaking my heart…and cutting me out of your life completely… (*Indicates* Vanity Fair) But here it is.

Silence.

I guess I owe you a thank you…(*Nods slowly*) And… maybe one day I'll give it to you. (*Beat*) But right *now*? The best I can give you…is a "go fuck yourself."

Pilots

• • •

Characters

PERSON: any age. Male or female.

Notes

Feel free to improvise and work off of the reactions from the audience.

Enters from offstage. Sees audience.

PERSON: Oh, perfect!

Walks quickly to the middle of the stage.

Hey, guys. If you don't mind, there's something I've been dying to tell people for years now, and I just *really* need to say it out loud. So…I'd appreciate it if you guys would just…ya know…let me get it off my chest. That cool? (*Beat*) Okay…

Closes eyes. Takes a deep breath. Shakes out hands. Braces themselves. Opens eyes.

I'm Kanye West…

Exhales sharply with a large smile. Relaxes completely as a huge weight comes off of their shoulders.

Oh, *man*! (*Laughs*) Whew! I've been waiting to say that for *years*! *God*, that feels good! (*Laughs with a shake of the head*) Thank you. Really. *God*, it feels like this… *burden* is finally *lifted* off of me! (*Sighs happily*) Now…I know you're probably thinking, "This person's crazy." right? Or like, "*Cleeaarly* that's not Kanye West! Kanye West doesn't *smile*!" (*Laughs. Deadly serious*) No, but seriously…I'm Kanye West. (*Beat*) Not *physically*, of course…but I'm everything that makes Kanye… *Kanye.* You see…I'm what is known in the industry as a "pilot"…and Kanye…is a "host." Think of it this way…most of the popular singers today have people who write their songs for them, right? Same goes for authors who hire ghostwriters. Well…now that you don't even *need* talent to be famous…there are people who write entire *careers*! (*Nods with a grin*) Pilots. I mean, we do it *all*! Write over-the-top award speeches, create idiotic fashion trends, pick out their kids' silly-ass names…basically, anything to keep them in the spotlight. Sounds complicated, right? (*Laughs heavily*) It's the easiest fucking job I've ever had in my *life*! And *I've* worked at Hollister! Like, okay…this one time, Kanye had a recording session coming up, and he asked me to write some lyrics for it. And…just as a *joke*…(*Beat*) I smashed my hands against my laptop with a Word document opened up…ya know, all sorts of gibberish and consonants. I turned it in…and guess what? That became the *Yeezus* album! And that shit went *platinum*! I'm telling you…you'd be *amazed* at the number of people who hire pilots to run their careers: Kim Kardashian? That's just a guy named Dirk in Bozeman, Montana! Great guy actually. Charlie Sheen! *His* pilot's an eighty-year-old woman from the Bronx! She used to be the pilot for Lindsay Lohan, Paris Hilton, *and* Carson Daly…at the same time! Lady's a *legend*! And it's not just *people* who hire pilots. All of Fox News is run by three professors from *MIT.* I'm *serious*! They created this *giant* keyboard with different hot-button topics on each key that covers the entire floor! Then...every day, they release about two dozen kittens and just go *apeshit* with laser pointers! (*Laughs*) *Right!* (*Shakes head with a smile. Sighs sadly*) But...as easy as it was with *Yeezey*... it had its downsides. I mean...I was never invited to any of the parties...I was on call twenty-four seven... and...sometimes...I actually had to speak to the guy. So...I recently said good-bye...(*Beat*) But...it's for the best, ya know? Besides! I've already got another pilot gig lined up. It's perfect! It pays *double* what I got with Kanye, I'm *never* on call, *and* it requires even *less* effort and attention! The only downside is...(*Beat*) I actually have to *tell* people that I work for Donald Trump...

House

• • •

Characters

PERSON: Any age. Male or female.

PERSON: Not even a *week* after I sign the paperwork, the realtor tells me we can't move forward with the sale until a family member does a final walk-through of the house. And seeing as I *am* the only family member…I gotta go *aaallll* the way back for…what…*two* minutes of work? Don't get me wrong…I feel terrible that I'm selling it. 'Cause… it's not *just* a house, ya know? My family's lived there for close to a century! So, selling it wasn't the *easiest* decision to make. But what other choice did I have? Uproot my life and move all the way back out there for family *history*? And with the market the way it was, renting it would've been a nightmare. So, no. It had to go. (*Beat*) I fly out there, get a taxi straight to the house, and I have it wait for me…'cause I'm only gonna be a minute, and then it's *right* back to the airport. But when I pull up to the front of the house…I notice that it looks…different. Nothing I can put my finger on…just that it almost looks a bit more… I don't know…*grim*. Like there's a shadow looming over it, ya know? I mean…it's an old house…it's always been a little creepy. But it looks a bit off. I go in the house… and the front room is *freezing*. A hell of a lot colder than it should be. I just brush it off as something *else* I have to deal with, and I continue through the house. But then…it starts getting *colder*…and I start getting that…*feeling*. You know…when you can *feel* someone's looking at you? Like you're being watched? So, now I start getting creeped out. I rush to the staircase to have a quick look upstairs, put my hand on the railing…and as I go to put my foot on the first stair...I swear to God...(*Beat*) I can't move. It's like I'm frozen in place. And I thought, "What the fuck?" Ya know? And then...the house starts creaking...or what *sounds* like creaking...(*Beat*) But then...it starts sounding like...*words*. I'm not fucking with you, okay? I'm *frozen* there, my foot hanging in midair...and I hear, "We know why you're here...we know what you've done." And it just keeps saying, "We know why you're here...we know what you've done." (*Beat*) All of a sudden...the voices stop. My body relaxes. And it doesn't feel cold anymore. (*Beat*) I ran out of that house so fucking fast...almost ripped the door off the goddamned taxi! (*Beat*) But I'll tell ya what... glancing back as we drove away? I swear to *God* that house seemed to have a brighter look to it...like it was laughing...

Silence.

So, uh...if you know anyone who's looking for a house to rent...just let me know, okay?

Laughs lightly. Face quickly turns back to serious. Looks away.

SuperForce

• • •

Characters

PAT: any age. Male or female.

PAT WALKS TO THE MIDDLE of the room, with a clipboard in hand. Gives a bright smile as they walk to their spot.

PAT: Good morning, recruits! It's great to have you all here! I, uh…I hope the teleportation beam wasn't too uncomfortable. It's brand new and…well…not *entirely* legal. But the agency's pretty confident it won't liquefy anyone… *again.* (*Laughs goofily*) I'm just kidding, kinda. *Anyhoo…* my name is *Pat.* I'm the recruitment officer for our government's Hero Division. Now…I know what you're thinking…(*Fists on hips*) "Hey, Pat! There's no such *thing* as a Hero Division!" Well…that's 'cause it's top secret! With the amount of money we spend on memory wipes, I sure as hell *hope* you've never heard of us! (*Laughs goofily*) You've all been brought here because the Hero Division has deemed your set of skills or powers a potential asset to the planet and are offering you a chance to try out for a certain…*supergroup…*(*Smiles*) You may have heard of 'em…(*Whispers*) *SuperForce.* (*Beat*) Holy shit, right? And you're probably thinking something like, "Whoa-whoa-*whoa*! Pat! You mean *the* SuperForce? With the flying guy, the muscly lady, and the rodent dude?" And to you, I say…you bet your sweet ass. Now…I can't confirm or deny whether or not any of them will be here today, so… don't ask! My lips are sealed! And to the few telepaths in the group today, don't any of you try getting in my head and…

Pretends to have someone messing around in their head.

Oh! *Oh!*

Pokes head with a finger.

Hey! Get outta there! (*Laughs goofily. Waves hand.*) I'm just kidding...(*Points to head*) I've got a microchip in here blocking your powers; you can't actually read my thoughts. *So!* Let's go over the schedule for the day and get started, shall we?

Flips a few pages on the clipboard.

At oh-nine-hundred hours, you'll all be off to the medical bay for your physicals. We'll also be testing your resistance to fire, for any signs of alien DNA in your bloodstreams, and, of course, for hypoglycemia. *Then*, at eleven hundred hours, it's on to the mental tests. You'll all be placed in separate rooms and given a few brief videos to watch as we study your responses. Videos range from a kitten chasing a butterfly, kids on a swing set, your family members being brutally tortured and screaming for their lives in one of our top-secret facilities...it *varies!* Now...at thirteen hundred hours, you will all be placed inside our militarized training maze. We call it...the Death Box. Live ammunition rounds *will* be used...along with flame throwers, spinning blades, throwing stars, and lava pits. For those of you who make it out alive, you will move on to the final event of the day...

Stares at the room seriously.

Our wine mixer! Now, if rumors are true, Becky in catering ordered us those *delicious* little bacon-wrapped date things? *God*, I love those! (*Beat*) Okay...let's see.

Scans the next few pages on the clipboard.

What else, what else...da-da-da-da-*daaa*...(*Beat*) Oh! Right! As you might have noticed...when you were all beamed here...a *ring* was placed on your middle finger. Now, this is no *ordinary* ring. It's also a communicator, a high-resolution camera, a short-range Taser...and, uh...my *personal* favorite...

Lifts a hand and clicks a light on and off on their own ring.

(*Giddy*) It's-got-a-little-flashlight-in-there! There's a little button on the side here. Pretty cool, huh? Oh, and it's also geared with the world's top voice-recognition technology, so all of these features work with voice commands! And, uh...*side note*...if you happen to...*tell* anyone another hero's identity or...a secret government location...or...well...not obey any direct order from any higher-up government official…it *kiiiinda* self-detonates the thermal grenade planted inside of it. Soooo…(*Finger guns*) *Don't-do-that!* (*Laughs goofily*) Well…I think that's pretty much it! I look forward to seeing which one of you will be the first recruit to finish this tryout alive! Any questions?

Five Stages of Grief

• • •

Characters

DAN: late twenties/early thirties

Notes

"Shivago" by Ludovico Einaudi helped me write this. It may help you perform it.

Darkness. Silence.

Lights slowly rise. Wind blows. Dried leaves rustle in swaying trees, unseen. DAN enters. He stops in the middle of the stage, facing us. His hands in the pockets of his jacket. Silence.

DAN: Hi.

Silence.

I, uh…I know it's been a while since I've, uh…made it out here. Things've been kinda tough these last few months. Tougher than normal, I mean. Haven't really been my best…(*Smiles lightly*) I know you'd tell me that's a terrible excuse…and you're right. And…I'm sorry.

Silence. Looks in the air, thinking.

I'm trying to think of what I told you the last time I was here. So much has happened. (*Beat*) I've started working again. Picking up a few gigs here and there. Just to keep my mind busy. It's, uh…it's okay…(*Shifts feet. Looks at the ground*) I've started seeing a therapist. I know…crazy, right? I told them that I was fine…that I didn't need one. (*Beat*) My therapist tells me that's called denial…the first stage of grief.

Silence.

I've started talking to your mom on the phone. That's my homework assignment each week for therapy. Talk to Susan. "Did you talk to Susan this week? What did you and Susan talk about?" (*Smiles*) It's actually not that bad. It was a bit awkward at first...but now we've become real buddies. You probably would've hated it. (*Laughs*) It's great...we talk about everything. Though we usually end up talking about you...(*Beat*) We usually cry. (*Beat*) She misses you more than you'd probably believe. (*Beat*) And so do I.

Silence.

Ya know, I...I think you would've been proud of me. I was doing really well for a while. I mean...I still felt like I was constantly *drowning*, but...I thought that maybe I was past the worst of it...

Looks down. Rubs the palm of his hand with the other hand's thumb—a nervous tick.

Then, uh...about two months ago...I woke up...and I looked over at your side of the bed...(*Beat*) And I couldn't stop staring at how...*empty* it was. And I...I just started *bawling*. I cried my eyes out till I got sick. (*Beat*) After that...it was like I was looking through a fog every single day. I'd be eating dinner and instinctively glance up to look at you…and I'd lose it. I woke up in the middle of the night once and saw that I interlocked my own hands…thinking one was yours. (*Beat*) I could barely get out of bed, I stopped going to therapy, I'd forget to call your mom or be too upset to answer her calls…

Silence.

I was in a really bad place…and I couldn't stop hurting, ya know?

Silence.

But then I got a call from your mom. A *dozen* calls actually. She wouldn't *stop* calling till I picked up. She tells me…that Meg's in town, and she's bringing the girls. "Get off your ass, and clean yourself up…they're begging to see their uncle Danny!" (*Beat*) So, I, uh…I cleaned the house…tried to put myself together a bit… (*Beat*) God, I was so nervous…I hadn't seen the girls in over a *year*. They weren't at the funeral, so…(*Smiles sadly*) But there they were. So happy and just…full of energy. God…Maddy's so big now; you wouldn't believe it. She looks *just* like Meg, it's crazy. But, uh…but the craziest thing…was seeing Emma…(*Fights back tears*) She looks *just* like you. Like your little doppelganger. (*Beat*) And it's not just the looks either. She's got your laugh…and, uh…your dry sense of humor…and…Meg was telling me that…she likes holding someone's hand while she sleeps…just like you. (*Beat*) And she has no problem being bossy, so you two are *definitely* related. (*Laughs*)

Silence.

Meg was worried that seeing her would make me feel worse. But…believe it or not…it was exactly what I needed. Knowing that there's someone out there…someone that fills the world with even a *part* of what you gave it…that made me so happy.

Looks at feet. Silence.

My, uh…my therapist says…that this is the *final* stage of grief. (*Beat*) That, uh…acceptance doesn't mean that I'm *cured* or anything. That the feeling of loss will be with me forever. It just means that I can begin readying myself…to *try* and move on.

Nervous tick.

And, uh…I guess…I just wanted to let you know that, uh…(*Looks at the grave*) I'm gonna *try*, now…okay? (*Smiles softly. Whispers*) Okay.

Contact Information

• • •

Website: MatthewMclachlan.com
E-mail address: MMclachlan123@gmail.com

CPSIA information can be obtained at www.ICGtesting.com
Printed in the USA
BVOW04s2138050916

461212BV00002B/85/P

9 781535 054171